This Sporting Life

GOLF

Bill Elliott

This Sporting Life

GOLF

The story of the men and women
who made the game what it is today

DAVID & CHARLES

A DAVID & CHARLES BOOK

First published in the UK in 1998

Copyright © Bill Elliott 1998

Bill Elliott has asserted his right to be identified as author
of this work in accordance with the Copyright, Designs
and Patents Act, 1988.

A catalogue record for this book is available from the
British Library.

ISBN 0 7153 0602 2

Printed in Italy by Milanostampa SpA
for David & Charles
Brunel House   Newton Abbot   Devon

This book is dedicated to the memory of journalist and author

PETER DOBEREINER

who tried to teach me about golf but taught me rather more

about life, the universe and red wine

Foreword

Golf is many things to many people. To some it is no more than a pleasant way to perambulate through retirement and on to The Great Fairway in the Sky. To others it is an obsession, a magnificent triviality, a game that curls itself around at least the outer reaches of a genuine philosophy. This is golf as Zen.

Meanwhile for professionals golf has never been more lucrative, the major stars earning increasingly staggering amounts of money for their time and their skill so that they do not perambulate at all; instead this elite group circumnavigates the globe in private jets, a small army of attendants looking after their every whim.

For most of us who play the game, however, the attraction is more complex. First there is the challenge. No sport offers greater opportunities for personal triumph and disaster than golf. Even the blandest of rounds can suddenly offer up the chance for a player to produce the shot of his or her life, the three wood over a lake, the pitch and putt par on a hole that hitherto had caused nothing but anguish. Equally a player can find out everything there is to know about his own character, some of which he may not particularly wish to pass on to anyone else.

Then there is the social side, the camaraderie that comes from a shared experience that usually takes place in a beautiful setting. Mark Twain may have felt that golf 'was a good walk spoiled' but for many millions of us he is spectacularly wrong. For us golf is a good walk made infinitely better. Certainly over the years I have strolled with deer and pheasant, gazed in wonder at an eagle swooping overhead and once delayed teeing off at a hole in South Africa for half an hour while my companion and I sat entranced while watching a troop of monkeys put on the greatest acrobatic display in history no more than 10 yards away.

I have sweltered in Florida, shivered in Ireland, been threatened by a snake in Arizona, almost died after a wasp sting in Carolina and played in to the haunting sound of a lone piper at St Andrews. I have won, lost and halved matches, played stone cold sober and badly, as well as dead drunk and well. I have, however, never been bored and I have made some real friends because of golf more than I ever did playing football, rugby, cricket or tennis. I also make my living writing about the game, its eccentricities, its superstars, its somehow magical allure, and so when my editor, Sue Viccars, asked me if I was interested in writing this book I was able to agree immediately. The idea of exploring the recent past of the sport is a compelling one for at the turn of the twentieth century much has changed – and is changing – about the grand, old game.

The men and women I have interviewed have seen these changes take place at close-quarters over the second half of this century. Golf has grown, become more democratic and certainly more commercial. Parts of it have become a huge, corporate bandwagon that at times is not a hugely pleasant sight, and yet the core values remain unsullied. There is still an expectation in golf that a player will supervise himself, that civility is expected and that a round that does not end in a sporting handshake has not really taken place at all. There is no equivalent in golf to the professional foul, no condoning of shabby behaviour. If this reads as stuffy then so be it but in my experience stuffiness in golf resides only in some clubhouses and never out on the course.

So much remains the same now as it was at the beginning of the century although this is a bit like saying because cars still have four wheels they too have not moved on much. No, the fact is that while the basic principles of golf are as unwavering now as they were 100 years ago the sport has evolved as much as, say, a Porsche 911 Turbo compared to a Model-T Ford. What I have tried to do in this book is to provide snapshots in time through the eyes and ears of those men and women who can remember what it was like to play the game as a pro or who had to caddie to put bread on a table or who once walked behind a horse mowing a fairway. Their memories are, inevitably, disparate and eclectic but as they talked their affection for golf shone through constantly.

Sometimes I have had to correct certain details, a name here, a place there, but for the overwhelming part the words belong, rightly, to them. For example I was advised by Peter Alliss that golf writer Mark Wilson had got it wrong when he claimed a certain draft game ended because a blonde spotted a condom in her gin and tonic. According to Peter it ended when the offending object surfaced in the Mayor of Altrincham's pre-dinner drink. I am sure Peter is right – after all, he admits to being one of the players involved at the time – but I have left Wilson's story as he told it precisely because it was how Mark remembered it. Anyway it is only a game or, if I may paraphrase P. J. O'Rourke, golf is so damn good because it combines two of mankind's favourite pastimes... taking long walks and occasionally hitting things with a stick.

Finally I have included descriptions of what I consider to be the world's more interesting courses. The only two rules governing this eclectic listing is that a) I had to know the courses personally, and b) no one was allowed to dispute my choices. You may notice that there are fourteen of them which, coincidentally, is what I believe should be the maximum number of holes on a course simply because of a lifelong habit of allowing what passes as my game to fall apart over the 15th, 16th, 17th and 18th.

BILL ELLIOTT, *Rowledge, 1998*

Chapter 1:
The Professional Game

'His type come and go each year'

American sportswriter Charlie Price quoting his editor's response when he suggested writing a feature on Arnold Palmer

The Professional Game

Golf professionals have been around for at least 200 years although life for them back then was not quite as we know it now. Indeed until the latter half of the nineteenth century the professional was more often than not a decent player who really earned his daily money by greenkeeping, making and repairing clubs and constructing feathery, subsequently guttie, golf balls.

Old Tom Morris, the most famous professional of his day, for example, not only learned to play the game at St Andrews, he was a greenkeeper both there and at Prestwick. The fact that he helped set up the first Open Championship at Prestwick in 1860 and went on to win the title four times brought him fame, lots of glory and very little money. His son, also named Tom, became even more famous when he won The Open four times in a row, before dying at just twenty-four years of age from a broken heart a few months after his wife died in childbirth.

Nowadays, of course, Old and Young Tom would have been multi-millionaire superstars, flying in their own jets, lauded and applauded everywhere they went. This, however, is a modern phenomenon. The harsh fact is that although professionals in the first half of the twentieth century could make reasonable money, their social status was still that of the artisan. It may seem ludicrous now but when Henry Cotton was winning Open Championships he was still denied access to most clubhouses.

Cotton, who was always financially astute, was rich enough eventually to own a home in London's Eaton Square and happily underlined his wealth by employing a butler. Wonderfully, he further consoled himself by occasionally having this butler serve him lunch from a Fortnum & Mason's hamper while he sat in his Rolls-Royce in a club car-park between rounds at a tournament. As a gesture of contempt at the rampant snobbery of the day this was supreme and the attendant publicity helped raise the status of the touring professional at least. The club pro, however, was still expected to remain 'downstairs' while members gathered at the clubhouse bar.

Gaining entry to the clubhouse, however, was never really a problem for Bernard John Hunt. The man who was to go on to become one of the finest golfers of his generation, and twice a Ryder Cup captain, neatly side-stepped any restrictions on entry by arranging to be born inside one on 2 February 1930. This was at Atherstone Golf Club in Warwickshire and happily occurred because Hunt's father was the club professional at the time. 'I was,' he recalls with some pride, 'born *upstairs*.'

He was also inevitably immersed in golf as he grew up. There was never really a conscious decision on his part to become a pro, rather a sort of drip-drip osmosis took place so that when he showed a genuine talent for the game his future career was confirmed without the tiresome necessity of much soul-searching or even a little conversation.

'My father was not only the professional, he also did some work on the course itself which was quite the norm at many clubs in those days. And, of course, I helped him. In fact I grew up doing everything. I'd driven a tractor years before I should have, worked behind the bar at a young age, even cut the bread, buttered it and served scones and tea to members when Mum was not around for whatever reason. But I also had the time to practise as much as I wanted. And how I wanted to practise. I'd been born into golf, you see. In fact, really, I'd been born a professional. From the start this is what I wanted to do, what I worked towards and applied myself to achieving.'

By the time he was sixteen years old, Hunt had embraced at least the first part of his ambition. He was a professional, a title achieved by simply having two other established pros propose and second his application to join the Professional Golfers' Association. Thus began a career for Hunt that continues today on the Seniors' Tour.

It is a career that is studded with tournament successes. In Europe, Hunt won the likes of the Belgian, German and French Opens, while in Britain he was a

Above: 'Young' Tom with The Open Championship Belt
Right: 'Old' Tom Morris with 'Young' Tom Morris Jnr

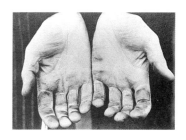

Left: The always elegant Cotton pictured in 1946

Right: Cotton' hands showing the places where the club contacts, 1937

consistent winner of titles that now are as redolent of the past as one of those Hovis commercials on television. Tournaments like the Gleneagles–Saxone, the Swallow–Penfold and the Gallaher Ulster. Somehow they do not make them like that any more.

Yet when Hunt set off on his great adventure shortly after World War II there was no structured circuit on which to play and certainly no experienced group of tournament professionals from whom he could learn the ropes. In the 1950s he was competing against professionals whose real job was running a club shop and whose forays into tournament play were erratic at best.

'I never had an amateur career, indeed I never regarded myself as an amateur. Golf to me was always a means of making money, a job, certainly not a pastime. All those years watching my father at work made sure

of that. But I was anxious to make my living from actually playing the game.'

The inspiration for this outrageous ambition came from across the Atlantic in America where a more sophisticated commercial approach meant there were many professionals making a good living from tournament play without the drudgery of then having to sell tee pegs over the counter in a club shop. Back in Britain, Hunt was so rare as to need protection. But he was not alone, for an equally young and ambitious golfer called Peter Alliss had decided to try the same route to fame, glory and money. Like Hunt, Alliss's father was a professional golfer. In fact Alliss senior was an outstanding player, good enough to play in three Ryder Cups. Until Spain's Ignacio Garrido followed his father Antonio into Ryder Cup battle when he played for Europe against the USA in 1997, Percy and Peter

Bernard Hunt meets the Press, a rather more sedate affair than today's mass-media conferences

> 'Peter and I were the only two at that time who were making a living playing tournament golf so it really was quite an adventure for us.'

were the only father and son to have taken part in the famed match.

As Bernard Hunt sat in the study of his comfortable Surrey home to talk about his life, the warmth of his smile when he mentioned Peter Alliss was obvious. Right from the start these two men, Hunt older by one year, forged a friendship that remains vibrant to this day, a friendship that began because they were treading new sporting turf all those years ago.

'Peter and I were the only two at that time who were making a living playing tournament golf so it really was quite an adventure for us. We'd done our National Service first, of course, so we were both champing at the bit to play golf. Even then there were quite a few tournaments to play, most of them sponsored by companies already in the golf business or by newspapers. The *Daily Mail*, the *News of the World* and the *Yorkshire Post* all had tournaments back then.'

The money for someone like Hunt who not only had ability but was willing to travel was surprisingly good. In 1953 he won his first big-time professional tournament, the Spalding, and before the year was over he had won four other titles. Suddenly the young man's bank account was looking very healthy indeed.

'It's always difficult to compare money now and then. Sure there is more now but it wasn't bad back then either. I'll give you a example. The first house my wife Meg and I bought was a four-bedroom job in Pinner. We had children by then so we also had a live-in girl to give Meg a hand when I was away, which I was a lot. I remember that house cost £5,000 and I paid for it out of my winnings that year. That same house now would be worth around £350,000 so there's a comparison for you. We had, I can assure you, a very nice lifestyle.

'I've never had any complaints about the sort of money I've earned. My first winner's cheque in 1953 was for £300. In fact I've always felt a little uneasy about it. Even now I think I'm overpaid on the Seniors Tour. Maybe that's one of the reasons why I never won a major championship like The Open, though I came close a couple of times. Maybe I was too comfortable, too content with my life. Certainly championship

winners like Tony Jacklin and Henry Cotton always seemed to be a lot more concerned with making lots of money than I ever was. Cotton used to moan about the money that Jacklin was making after he won The Open and the US Open in 1969–70, and Jacko was the same when Seve Ballesteros emerged. They were more driven somehow than I was. I remember when Peter was the subject of the television programme *This Is Your Life* and Jacklin was there to pay tribute, backstage he started moaning about how much Seve was making until I could stand it no longer.

'I said, "For Christ's sake, Tony, you once told me that after you won The Open, Mark [McCormack (pictured above), the lawyer, sports agent and founder of the phenomenally successful International Management Group] promised you would never have to struggle for money for the rest of your life". Jacko just looked at me and said, "Yeah, but Seve can buy his own plane or an island and I can't". I had to laugh but, looking back, maybe that was what drove them on to achieve more. I'm not sure.

'Certainly I never got the impression that Jack Nicklaus or Gary Player were that bothered about money although they've each made an awful lot of the stuff. But they always seemed just to want to win majors and Gary especially just wanted to play golf all the time. No one travelled more than him and I doubt anyone ever will. He went to America to play golf when he didn't have two bucks in his pocket. There was a big, posh party once and Gary only got in because a friend of his went in and then handed his jacket back out of a window so Gary could wear it to gain admittance. He was so hard-up back then that he couldn't even afford a jacket. You've got to admire him.'

Not content with trail-blazing in Europe, Hunt and Alliss also began to play tournaments in South America and South Africa. Air travel was becoming more organised and the two pals were determined to make the most of what was available. The world as far as they were concerned was their play-pen. While the majority

Left: Captain of the 1973 Ryder Cup team Bernard Hunt

Mark McCormack's first and most famous client Arnold Palmer, here aged 27 during his second season as a professional, ready for a practice round at Augusta

of their countrymen regarded the Isle of Man as a major overseas trip, Messrs Hunt and Alliss were quite happy to fly thousands of miles to play golf for weeks, sometimes months, at a time.

Then when Hunt picked up his playing rights to the US Tour the big man did not hesitate. By now he owned the club shop at the Hartsbourne Club in Hertfordshire but the deal he struck meant his father and brother ran it and did most of the teaching duties. 'I never wanted to teach back then. I have since, of course, but then I didn't want to spend my winters on the practice ground with pupils.'

Instead he spent them in California, in Palm Springs and in Arizona, driving vast distances across the USA, while back home the loyal Meg raised a family. Meanwhile Hunt's eyebrows were raised when he took a flight to New York after competing in the 1958 US Masters at Augusta National in Georgia. It was a night flight and Hunt found himself sitting next to Mark McCormack. Big Mac's first and most famous

client Arnold Palmer had just won his first Masters and McCormack, ever the workaholic, spent the flight finishing off Palmer's tax returns.

'Finally Mark shut the books and turned to me with a satisfied smile. "D'you know," he said, "with all his taxes and expenses paid, Arnold has just cleared a million dollars for the year." I honestly couldn't think of a reply. Then Mark mentioned that one of Arnold's sponsors was a tile manufacturer. It was the first time I realised that there could be sponsors from businesses unconnected with golf. That was a real eye-opener at the time.'

Earning a million back in Europe was not quite so easy although a first victory in Italy at least made him a lira millionaire at the time. 'The Continental events were fun as well as paying quite well. Players were always treated splendidly over there and it wasn't long before £1,000 first prizes were fairly common. That was really quite sensational money because expenses for the week would never be more than around £40.'

The number of players competing was similar to today on the European Tour but of the 150 teeing up against Hunt only a handful ever really stood a chance of beating the likes of himself and Alliss, the majority of contestants being club pros who played only a few tournaments each year.

The galleries, however, were often very different from today and not just because they tended to wear belted raincoats no matter what the weather was like. Television was still in its infancy so that if a fan wished to see a player perform he or she had little option than to pay at the gate. It was, of course, harder to travel because of an antiquated road system and fewer cars, so tournaments in Britain were spread around geographically and each was supported enthusiastically by the local population. It is the highest of ironies that despite golf's burgeoning popularity over the last twenty-five years there was much more high-level professional golf to witness in the British Isles when Hunt and his rivals were in action.

And, at least as far as Hunt is concerned, the interest from the media in the game 'was probably better than it is now. Certainly it was more about the game whereas now it all seems to be about personalities. Crowds, too, were big, at least as big as they are now. There is no doubt that the Ryder Cup has grown in many ways but it was a big deal in my day as well. I recall Meg and I walking up the steps at Lindrick [the Yorkshire club where Great Britain & Ireland won in 1957] and gasping in astonishment when we looked back and saw the crowds assembled there. Mind you, I'm not sure how much longer there will be crowds at golf tournaments. Maybe always at the Ryder Cup but my own suspicion is that television, and particularly the introduction of digital TV, will do away with many of them.

'No one is keener on the Ryder Cup than I am but I didn't bother going out to Spain in 1997. At Oak Hill two years earlier I ended up watching most of the play on television. Perhaps the time is not too far away when spectators will be allowed in for nothing at golf events, just to provide some atmosphere for the television cameras.'

The Ryder Cup has been a constant and golden thread running through Hunt's career. He first played in the biannual match in 1953 and took part on seven other occasions between then and 1973 when he took over as captain, a duty he repeated two years later at Laurel Valley in Pennsylvania. During all this time it was Great Britain & Ireland versus the mighty United States, a David and Goliath situation that almost invariably ended in victory for the Americans and which eventually led to Great Britain & Ireland becoming Europe in 1979 so that players like Ballesteros might enter the fray. Back in 1953, however, a young Hunt was thrilled as well as surprised to make the team that year.

During the 1953 Ryder Cup the team were billeted at The Dormie House at Sunningdale

Christy O'Connor, 'Himself', playing in the Ryder Cup at Lindrick in 1957

Selection was made by the executive committee of the Professional Golfers' Association in tandem with the team captain. In 1953 this was Henry Cotton and as far as Hunt was concerned the aloof Englishman was an aristocrat of the game. Pausing only to purchase what he describes as a 'sporting suit' from Daks, Hunt made his way to the Wentworth Club in Surrey to meet the great man and prepare to play against the USA in October 1953. Cotton was waiting for him outside the clubhouse and the initial exchange between the captain and his rookie player perhaps lacked some of the psychology we now associate with high-octane sport. 'How do you do?' said Cotton stiffly as he extended a hand. 'Very well thank you, Mr Cotton,' replied Hunt. This was the sort of deference Cotton liked but it was easy enough for Hunt to manufacture at the time.

'I was in awe of him. It's as simple as that. There is no way that I could have addressed him as anything but mister,' he says. Mr Cotton then introduced young Mr Hunt to a life he never really knew existed. The team was billeted in The Dormie House at Sunningdale Golf Club a few miles down the A30 from Wentworth and here Hunt, Alliss and the other six members of the Great Britain & Ireland side were issued with team uniforms, blazers, flannels, shirts and slacks and, of course, specially made golf bags. Hunt could cope with this all right but when steak was served for supper that evening he was more than slightly pleasantly shocked. 'It was still in the days of food rationing, and steaks were not exactly something you expected to see on a menu. But Henry had arranged for steaks to be delivered every day for us to eat. He claimed it would be the difference between us winning and losing. And maybe it was.'

Today's Ryder Cup is played over three days – fourballs, foursomes, fourballs, foursomes, followed by the singles – play starting shortly after dawn and finishing at dusk between twelve-man teams. The eight-man sides of 1953, however, adopted a rather more leisurely approach to the affair, staged over two days with the foursomes first, followed the next day by the singles. Hunt admits he was nervous but if the opening day (he

Left: 1948 British Open Champion Henry Cotton, Muirfield

lost) was a bitter disappointment, the singles proved even more traumatic, particularly for Alliss.

Great things were expected from the two young English lions but each lost in the foursomes, steak or no steak, and it then turned into spam-fritter time in the singles. Alliss, just twenty-two, was sent out in the sixth match by Cotton, Hunt down to play in seventh place. Each could have won their match and if either had managed a victory then the Americans would have been beaten, but each fumbled over the closing hole, Alliss fluffing an awkward pitch off a tight lie and under the most exquisite pressure. Cotton, watching from the side, was furious and stalked off. Poor Alliss was mortified.

'I saw Peter make a mess of the hole from behind. It was a shame because I think he'd led all the way but, you know, these things happen. I didn't do any better

> O'Connor's ability to consume alcohol like the devil on a
> binge but still play golf like an angel was the stuff of legend.

in my match but I was less affected by it than Peter. I remember walking into the clubhouse and Cotton coming over to me and just asking "How did *you* do?". It wasn't a great moment really. Peter, meanwhile, came in for a lot of criticism, 'the man who lost the Ryder Cup', and that sort of thing but, really, no one was harder on Peter than he was himself. He took it very badly. Indeed it still affects him. He felt he'd lost face because he really was a hell of a good player.'

Four years later Hunt and Alliss felt rather differently when they helped Great Britain & Ireland to an historic victory at Lindrick in Yorkshire. This naturally was an inspirational moment, but perhaps the most inspired moment of Hunt's entire career came some sixteen years later when he captained the Ryder Cup team at Muirfield. By now the match was closer in composition to the modern spectacular except that the opening two days of foursomes and fourball play was then followed by morning and afternoon singles on the final day. This, even for seriously committed golfers, was desperately tiring. And no one felt more exhausted at lunch-time on the last day than Ireland's legendary Christy O'Connor.

O'Connor, affectionately and universally known simply as 'Himself', was forty-eight years old and although his ability to work the ball any which way he wished was still firmly in place, the old bones were starting to creak a little. In the morning singles, he had disappointingly lost to J. C. Snead, and that, Christy decided, was enough. As he walked past Hunt towards

the clubhouse he announced that he would prefer not to play in the afternoon. This was not a problem really because only eight players were required to do duty out of a ten-man team. But the skipper had decided he wanted the old war-horse to have one more round. Unfortunately this was exactly what O'Connor fancied as well, only in his case it was to be at the bar.

Now, O'Connor's ability to consume alcohol like the devil on a binge but still play golf like an angel was the stuff of legend so Hunt was not too bothered when he noticed that Christy seemed to be taking lunch of a liquid variety. He charged O'Connor's wife Mary with getting Christy to the tee on time and then formulated a scheme that now would make banner headlines in the tabloids for all the wrong reasons.

'Obviously I knew Christy very well and I knew that he could, if necessary, play stunning golf with a few drinks under his belt but I knew also that if the alcohol started to run out of his system, he could struggle. My plan was simple: I pulled aside a couple of his pals, one of them was a priest, and said, "Whatever happens, keep him topped up". To this end we made sure there was going to be a tot available on every tee. By the time Christy came down to play he was clearly, shall we say, happy.'

The other person to notice this was O'Connor's opponent that afternoon. A few months earlier Tom Weiskopf had won The Open and he was incredulous as O'Connor appeared on the tee. Turning to Hunt the American asked, 'Has he been drinking?' Hunt, to his credit, never turned a hair. Instead he replied, 'Yes, and if we can keep him that way then you don't stand a chance.'

This, as it happened, turned out to be half right, the ageing Irishman and the new, young star of American golf halving their match after a thrilling contest. It is perhaps the most vivid contrast between pro golf then and now. This difference is not that the game was less serious then but that everyone had a more relaxed grip on the nonsense that is life. To put it another way, they just had a greater sense of fun.

Dai Rees holding the Ryder Cup played at Lindrick in 1957

Right: Bernard Hunt watches the flight of his ball while his caddie watches...the clubs!

While Bernard Hunt spent the latter years of his career as a club professional, combining his job at Foxhills Golf Club in Surrey from 1975 until he retired in 1994 with frequent forays on to the pro circuit, the vast majority of men who worked at, and for, a club lived far less glamorous lives. Although most started out embracing the usual dream of winning major championships the harsh fact is that very few golfers are equipped either technically or emotionally for life on the golf tour. The constant travel, the drain on the nerves, the months spent away from family and friends meant that a natural culling took place so that teenage dreams soon gave way to the more practical requirement of having to earn a wage to put bread on the table and, sooner or later, shoes on the children's feet.

Bill Dawson is from the same generation as Bernard Hunt and each is a professional golfer, but there the similarity ends. While Hunt hurtled into pro golf as a tournament player right from the start of his career, the young Dawson took a rather more erratic route in earning a living from the game, playing for fun growing up in Scotland. To be fair he was a decent player, certainly enjoying a low single-figure handicap by the time he started his apprenticeship at a boat-building yard in Argyle. 'I thought that was going to be my job for life. Parents were always on at you in those days to get a trade because then you could get a job for ever more. Or so we thought. So I learned how to build wooden-hulled boats and if it hadn't been for National Service then I very much doubt I would have ever gone near a golf club except to play the game.'

National Service, of course, changed the lives of many young men throughout the fifties. For some it was merely a distraction before they returned to what they had been doing before their call-up, unchanged except that now they could march fairly well and some at least had learned how to sew a button on a shirt. For others, however, the opportunity to travel – even if this only meant leaving a small home town and moving to

Tom Williamson and his staff at Nottingham Golf Club in 1900

the lowest paid apprenticeship in the country.'

Peter Alliss and caddie 'Mullins' during The Sunningdale Foursomes in 1979

a larger one a few hundred miles away – plus the exposure to other young men whose upbringing and education may have been hugely different to their own, changed lives forever. There is a theory that the great socio-economic changes in the sixties were rooted in the National Service experience.

Whatever the truth of this, however, there is no doubt that the two years Bill Dawson spent in the RAF between 1953 and 1955 took him on to a different road and helped to create a very different life than he otherwise would have experienced. He had, he reckons, a handicap of five when he entered the Royal Air Force. Two years later this was down to three. Clearly National Service had benefited Dawson. Discovering the joys of button-sewing and improving a handicap by two strokes is worth two years of anyone's life. More significantly he became friends with a couple of other keen golfers who turned out also to have been assistant-professionals before hearing the call to arms in 1953.

'I'd never really thought about getting a job in golf before I met these guys, Denis Bailey and Barry Davies, who are golf pros to this day. But the idea certainly appealed to me. By then I'd completed my five-year apprenticeship at the boat-builders so I reckoned I'd give it a go when I came out of the RAF. If it didn't work out I always had my trade to fall back on.'

Thus inspired, he left RAF Lyneham near Swindon, soon afterwards applying for an assistant-professional's post at the East Berkshire Club. To his delight he was successful. He was, however, rather less pleased when he discovered what his wages were to be...

'Assistants in those days were glorified slaves. Certainly it was the lowest paid apprenticeship in the country. My base wage, my retainer, was £2 10s a week and the teaching and playing fees were 6s and 8s respectively. I was allowed to keep twenty-five per cent of these fees so it meant that I could teach for an hour and then keep 1s 6d. Even allowing for the difference in what money would then purchase, this was fairly desperate. I remember confronting my boss and telling him that I couldn't exist on this but he wouldn't budge. I could like it or lump it. His reasoning was that if I was out of the shop for an hour or so then I was no use to him so he needed recompensing. For the same reasons it was also frowned upon that you get married. It was general knowledge, for example, that Tommy Haliburton [then professional at the Wentworth Club in Surrey] refused to employ married assistants. The last thing those club pros wanted was for an assistant to have a wife back home wanting him to return at a regular hour.

'The club professional's attitude was that we were lucky to be learning the job and that we should dedicate our lives to it. It meant very, very long hours. In the winter this meant me cycling to work to start at eight and not finishing until six. In summer we started earlier and finished later. It meant working all the hours God sent, seven days a week. That's why I say we were treated like slaves. There was a certain amount of training but not much. Nowadays it is properly structured but back than it was haphazard and depended on what sort of pro an assistant ended up working for. A lot of assistants just picked stuff up as they went along.

'The golf pro is now made to be much more responsible by the Professional Golfers' Association; the whole training process is properly structured, but it was a completely different ball game back then. I'd have to wash the wheels on the trolleys when they came back in off the course. Now an assistant would laugh if I asked him to do such a menial task. It was the same with the pro's golf shoes. It'd be my responsibility to

o take four whole days for my honeymoon. Contrast that with my own
got married in September and took *three weeks* off.'

clean and shine them so they were always perfect for him to go out to play with members. The current crop would consider such a chore to be beneath them. And the idea of paying your boss a percentage of your money has gone, too. Now the assistants expect to play or teach five hours a day. Mind you it's for the better. I wouldn't want anyone to have to work long hours for the pittance I earned. Like many hundreds of others I only stuck it because I wanted so much to be a pro myself. For me it was a vocation, a calling if you like; it wasn't just a job.'

Part of this job, as it still is now, was learning how to repair and refurbish golf clubs. Clubs forty years ago were either wooden or, in the case of irons, steel. The wooden heads on drivers, two woods, three woods and so on were kept in place by yards of 'whipping' or pitched twine, wound tightly around the neck of the club. This was done by hand and is a real skill. Learning this skill as well as how to repair scratches or gouges in the highly polished wood took many hours. These skills are still taught today although with metal clubs now the norm, the old glue pot is needed only for those 'Luddites' who refuse to play with the latest technology.

Meanwhile Dawson and his colleagues also needed to learn much else, most notably how to be polite and deferential to club members. His assertion that assistants were 'slaves' may be over-egging the pudding but it was not too far wide of the mark when it came to social status. Certainly there was little in the way of over-familiarity or even simple friendliness when it came to how assistants and usually even the club professionals were treated. The fact is that if you had a forelock then you had to learn swiftly how to tug it.

'We were much more separate from the club than we are these days, much more on a par with the green-keeping staff. All my clubs have been traditional, private member clubs. After East Berkshire I moved to Sunningdale as First Assistant but the system was the same – assistants were not allowed into the clubhouse. At Sunningdale in those days even the pro [Arthur Lees, a player good enough to perform in the Ryder Cup] had only limited access. It was very much a "them and us" society and we were most definitely "them". As an

assistant, if you needed anything from the clubhouse then you went to the back kitchen door and waited. It was funny really because although we were very much "staff", because we could play the game better than most of the members we were granted at least a modicum of respect. Mind you sometimes it was a very grudging respect. You always got the occasional member who would bellow at you and only use your surname when he did it.'

Thankfully these insecure chaps were in a minority, albeit a vociferous one. To counterbalance the down-right rude approach, there were members who took a sincere interest in the development of many young professionals, recognising their greater skill with a golf club and demonstrating their sincerity by putting their hands deep into their pockets to help fund the assistants when it came to playing in tournaments. 'If I was playing in the Assistants Championship or similar then these guys would pass the hat round. We didn't have sponsors in those days, we had benefactors.'

During his time in the Air Force, Dawson's ambition soared beyond merely becoming an assistant-professional. Like millions before and since he harboured dreams of winning an Open or at least making his mark as a tournament professional even though such players were even fewer and farther between than they are these days.

'Yes, I'd love to have been a touring pro if only for a few years but it wasn't to be. The structure was not in place back then for one thing; maybe I was never quite good enough, maybe other things got in the way, like marriage for example and the need to make a more secure living. But whatever the reason I never realised that ambition. It's a disappointment now as I look back but it's not a *huge* disappointment. I played in lots of regional and national PGA events and I've still got that desire for competition even now which is why it's such a delight to play in some of the senior events that are available to guys like me. I fairly quickly realised that I'd never be an Open Champion or a Ryder Cup player and so I settled for the other option of becoming a club pro instead. This, I stress, is not settling for the easy option because the life of a club pro is a hard one in many ways and if I've one regret as I look back it is that I wasn't able to spend more time with Gladys and the kids.'

There was not even much time to be spent on things such as a honeymoon, never mind the children that were to follow Bill's marriage to Gladys. By the time this happy event occurred Dawson had risen to the heady heights of First Assistant at Sunningdale. This meant a little more money to compensate for the extra responsibility. The downside was that he had to work for the redoubtable Arthur Lees whose disciplinarian approach to the job was equalled only by his love of playing golf for a significant wager.

The Dawsons married on a Thursday and as Lees left the reception he turned to his young assistant and said, 'Good luck, see you on Monday then'. While Lees returned to Sunningdale the Dawsons set off for London and a few nights at the Strand Palace Hotel, taking in Harry Secombe at The Palladium and Peter Sellers in a play called *Brouhaha*. It was heady stuff for the young couple and Dawson's spirits were high when he returned punctually to work on Monday morning. There he discovered all was not at peace.

'The moment I walked in one of the other assistants warned me that Arthur was on the warpath. "The boss is going absolutely potty: he wants to know why you were not in over the weekend," he told me. I went upstairs to see the boss and he was fuming. I told him there had obviously been a misunderstanding and that he had clearly told me not to return until Monday. No matter how much I insisted this was what had happened he denied ever saying it. Eventually we left it there but I nearly lost my job because I'd dared to take four whole days for my honeymoon. Contrast that with my own assistant at Wildernesse recently. He got married in September and took *three weeks* off. I had to work eleven hours a day, seven days a week to cover for him because September is a busy month. It would have been no good me saying "You can't do that" because it was not like that in my day. Times have changed and so have expectations. Three weeks may have been a bit much but good luck to him.'

By 1959 Dawson had become a full-blown club pro at the Littlestone Club on the Kent coast. Typical of many clubs in this corner of the south-east, Littlestone was an ultra-traditional place, a sort of haven for upper-middle class males who saw it as not only a place to play the game but a chance to recreate the style and ambience of their various public schools. He was more often than not referred to as 'Dawson' and entry into the clubhouse was by invitation of a member only. In the four years they spent there Mrs Dawson made it into this hallowed place just once despite many days spent serving in the club shop while her husband taught or played with members. 'The majority of members didn't even know she existed I'm afraid.'

It was not all doom at this apparently gloomy place, however. He remembers with affection the glamorous figure of George Livanos, son of the then biggest ship-owner in Greece (and his sisters Eugenie and Christina who married Stavros Niarchos and Aristotle Onassis respectively) – who would roar up in his Ferrari and treat him like a real friend as they played golf together. Still, it came as a relief when in 1963 he moved to Wildernesse where he was to stay for the next thirty-four years until his retirement, a lengthy period by any standards but one which was based on job satisfaction at a club that has treated him well and of which he is now an honorary member.

Compared to Littlestone, the Wildernesse set-up bordered on the bohemian with Bill astonished to be asked during his interview how he would like to be addressed: would *Mister* Dawson be okay? Actually he settled on 'Bill' but there were other immediate differences, too. He was asked how many days off a week he wanted – one, but the shop was to remain open for seven – and he was granted the 'privilege' of dining in the clubhouse although, inevitably, he was required to wear a jacket and tie.

It was, he says, 'a real eye-opener. Littlestone was then and remains now a very old-fashioned club but the Wildernesse was different, certainly friendlier. To be honest I never really enjoyed my time at Littlestone but it offered the chance to be a club pro and I'm grateful to them for that. It was a stepping stone. I couldn't believe the difference between the two places. At

Wildernesse there were people who actually seemed interested in me and even wanted to know my Christian name.'

As the in-coming professional he was required to fit out the shop. Although by now his teaching fee had rocketed to 12s 6d an hour ('and I kept it all!'), the cost of putting this shop together was daunting.

'My entire bank balance was £140 when I moved but the answer to my problem was to go to the PGCA [Professional Golfers' Co-operative Association] which had been set up to buy golf equipment in bulk on behalf of its shareholders who were all club pros. It cost £10 to become a shareholder and I was then able to borrow just under £1,000 and spend it at the PGCA to buy stock from their warehouse in Putney. The PGCA no longer exists; it went under about twenty-five years ago, and it is a great shame, indeed a disgrace, that it went the way it did. Certainly it affected a great many club pros although now there are small groups of professionals banding together to buy stock and at least try to compete with the big golf retailers who are now set up all over the country.

'Mind you, buying stock back in those days was a lot simpler than it is now. There were only about four types of ball and maybe half-a-dozen different sets of clubs. Nowadays there are so many I couldn't begin to count them. Also we didn't carry clothing. People wore their gardening clothes to play golf in; now it's a fashion statement. Back then they dressed down for the game, not up, which is one of the reasons for the strict dress codes still in existence at most clubs for entering the clubhouse bar or dining room. We didn't even have rain suits. If it rained you pulled on a heavy sweater, raised your umbrella and just got wet. That all changed when colour television came in. Suddenly there were all these guys, like Jack Nicklaus for example, looking great in colourful clothes, and gradually the club golfer wanted to look like his hero even if he couldn't ever play like him.

'Now it's all marketing, marketing, marketing. An awful lot of club pros now are sophisticated shop-keepers more than anything else, sitting in front of their computer ordering up more gear. I'm exaggerating a bit but the truth is you're not really the friendly

The clubhouse at Sunningdale

golf pro any more, more a slick marketing man. It's not what I came into the game to do but I suppose some people will see it as progress. Me, I'm glad to be out of it. The club pro now is an entrepreneur first and a golfer second; we were the other way round. In my opinion it's now all got out of hand, it's turned into a cut-throat, dog-eat-dog industry. I came into golf for the romance of the game and the job. For me it's been a vocation. The fact that for a lot of the time I earned buttons doesn't matter. The other fact is that I'm sure people my age have seen the best of it...but maybe when you get to my age that's what you always think.'

Chapter 2: 'They also serve who only pace the yardage.'

'There were three things in the world that he held in the smallest esteem … slugs, poets and caddies with hiccups.'

P. G. Wodehouse, *Rodney Fails to Qualify*, 1924

Left: A study in mutual concentration. Palmer and British caddie 'Tip' Anderson at the 1978 Open at St Andrews

Right: Caddies at Augusta, 1989

The Caddie

Caddies are a much put-upon species. Anyone can say he is a caddie just as anyone can nominate himself as a cook. Just as the latter title does not guarantee the eggs will be scrambled correctly, the former does not mean that a man, or indeed a woman, will do more than merely pick up your bag and thereafter lug it disconsolately around 18 holes. The true caddie does much more.

At St Andrews I have experienced both types. Paul was a student at the ancient town's almost equally ancient university. A nice lad, he turned up for our round wearing a tweed jacket, corduroy trousers and a pair of startlingly blue suede shoes. He was full of enthusiasm at the beginning – the imminent prospect of folding money is, in my experience, one of the only three things in life to encourage a student towards enthusiasm – but as the weather turned from mild and dry to cold and wet the poor

> He was a true caddie, a man whose expertise was as invaluable and enlightening as a sherpa's to a climber tackling a Himalayan peak.

young chap gradually descended into moroseness, his shoes even more despondent-looking than his face. He did his job that day as best he could which is to say he picked up my bag and, more or less, kept pace with me. At the end I was happy to pay him his agreed fee but I could just as happily have paid a donkey. All Paul did that day was to take the strain out of my round.

The next time I played the Old Course, I hired a proper caddie, the sort of gnarled and knowledgeable man who had spent his life getting to know St Andrews intimately. This chap, naturally, cost more because he knew more. After a few holes of working out the intricacies of what passes as my game, he chose each club for me with care, pointed me in the right direction (this is not always obvious at St Andrews), took into consideration the wind direction and other variables pertinent to links golf and allowed me to swing at the ball. On the greens, capacious and threatening as ever on this most eccentric of courses, this caddie knew every twist and turn, each subtle borrow. He was, in other words, a true caddie, a man whose expertise was

as invaluable and enlightening as a sherpa's to a climber tackling a Himalayan peak.

Naturally, he was Scottish and although it is not necessary to be a Scot also to be a true caddie, there seems little historic doubt that the first caddies were indeed born north of the border. For this we have to thank the potent mixture of Mary, Queen of Scots and her French connection. By the time Mary married the Dauphin, later Francis II, in the sixteenth century, golf was already a passionate pursuit for many Scots. Indeed as early as 1457 King James had signed a decree of the Scottish Parliament that 'the futeball and golfe be utterlie cryed down and not to be used' because too many members of the citizen army were neglecting their compulsory archery practice in favour of these two games.

By the time Mary returned from France 100 years later the peace treaty between England and Scotland meant there was no longer such compelling reason for chaps to meet on the border and launch arrows at each other. Instead, the Queen's love for golf turned it into the most fashionable pastime for Scotland's leisured classes. As befitted the wife of the Dauphin, Mary had brought back to Scotland with her platoons of pages to help ease her way through life's troubled passage. These, of course, were cadets and when some of these lads were dragooned into carrying their Queen's clubs around various courses, the Scots soon managed to turn cadet into caddie and a tradition, as well as a name, was born. Some 400 years after Mary first trundled around with her cadet, another Scot, Willie Aitchison, could be found standing rather red-faced and certainly slightly embarrassed, outside the clubhouse of the Royal Birkdale Club.

This magnificent links on the Lancashire coast at Southport was the setting for the 1965 Open Championship, and Aitchison was there because he was caddie to American star and defending champion Tony Lema. As he waited with the golfer's bag outside

Tony Lema at St Andrews with the 1964 Open Trophy
Overleaf: Caddie boys on Montrose Links in 1880, some using clubs to beat for a shooting party

the clubhouse, Lema, a charismatic personality, jumped out of a car and motioned for the caddie to follow him inside. What Lema did not realise was that caddies were not allowed inside the clubhouse and when the commissionaire stopped Aitchison, Lema's reaction was both instant and angry.

'What's the problem,' he asked.

'Sorry, sir, but caddies are not allowed in here, sir,' replied the unfortunate commissionaire.

'Well,' said Lema who was carrying the Open trophy with him at the time. 'If he's not allowed through here with me then I'm back in that taxi and not only heading back where I came from but taking this trophy with me. You'd better get it sorted out.'

Startled officials swiftly conferred, discretion was wisely favoured and suddenly Aitchison found the main door to one of England's most hallowed clubhouses being swung open to allow him to follow Lema inside. It was both an historic as well as an intensely satisfying personal moment for the Glaswegian.

'I believe I was the first caddie ever to walk through that front door and it was all down to Tony Lema. I've fought all my life to help improve the caddies' lot, to improve our status generally, and that moment when I walked through that door was the beginning of the pay-back for all the effort,' says Aitchison.

Certainly that Monday morning in 1965 was a long way from Aitchison's beginnings as a caddie. He recalls that the first time he caddied was at Girvan on the Ayrshire coast in the 1930s. He did so because money was in desperately short supply back then and because his father and his uncles had already established a family tradition of helping the 'nobs' play golf. The Queen of Scots might have been long dead but golf was still largely the exclusive pursuit of those leisured classes.

'I was still in short trousers, just a wee boy, and I used to caddie at weekends and during school holidays. Given my family connection it seemed perfectly natural to do it. It was the landed gentry, more or less, who played golf in those days; it was a rich man's game. At least that's how we viewed it. And they didn't want to see caddies at all until they were on the course.

'In fact we were fenced in those days, stuck away out of sight somewhere, usually near the clubhouse. Caddies were there just to do what they were told to do. As far as I was concerned, caddying was just a thing my dad and his brothers did to pick up an odd shilling or two. I only learned much later that one of my uncles actually caddied for James Braid. [Braid, along with two other British players, Harry Vardon and J. H. Taylor, dominated golf so much around the turn of the century that the trio was known as The Great Triumvirate, winning sixteen Open Championships between them from 1894 to 1914.]

'My uncle's name was James Aitchison, although he was known as 'Tim', and all this only started to come out when I began to make a name for myself. Unfortunately he died before I could get the whole story out of him but it was fascinating to know there was such a strong family tradition at caddying.'

When Aitchison returned home after the war, he also soon returned to caddying as a means of supplementing his income. Although he had started as no more than 'a wee boy carrying a canvas bag around a course', by 1951 he felt confident enough to offer himself up for service during the Amateur Championship itself at St Andrews. Back then, The Amateur was almost as big a deal for the golfing public as The Open itself. For the caddies, however, it was much bigger.

'Back in the early fifties there were very professional events and no pro circuit. Sure, I caddied in The Open but it was nowhere near as important to me as The Amateur. To a caddy, The Amateur was far more important financially. There used to be a lot of gambling in it in those days; a hell of a lot of money used

Left: Sandy Herd (top left) with The Great Triumvirate: (clockwise from top right) J.H. Taylor, Harry Vardon and James Braid pictured at St Andrews in 1905

Willie Aitcheson with Lee Trevino sheltering from the rain at the 1980 Open at Muirfield

to change hands, and a caddy, if he did his job properly, would make good dough. I always worked with guys who liked to gamble and what with the practice rounds and everything, it was two weeks' work in one. The Open, by contrast, never had any gambling during practice and the last 36 holes were played out on one day so it never meant as much forty years ago.'

As he travelled to St Andrews in 1951, however, the last thing on Aitchison's mind was money. More important, as he stepped off the bus that evening, was where he was going to sleep. There was no question of a hotel or even a modest guest house. Aitchison was already an accomplished caddie but, as usual at this time, he was also broke.

'I bumped into a greenkeeper and he took pity on me and said he'd find me somewhere to kip. This turned out to be one of his sheds. This one was behind the 14th hole. It's still there now but these days it's been converted into a toilet. Anyway, this decent guy brought me a bale of straw on which to lay my sleeping bag, some wood and coal to make a fire, and the next morning he turned up with some eggs and milk. This is how my professional caddying days started.'

After cooking his eggs and drinking his milk, Aitchison made his way to the first tee. Or rather he made his way to the caddies' pen, tucked away out of sight of the public and players. Caddies, or many of them at least, were still a motley crew nearly fifty years ago. While some were like Aitchison and aware of the growing need to behave at least vaguely professionally, the majority were little more than travelling men, closer to tinkers than the modern-day caddie. The clothes they wore were their own street clothes and they had usually slept in them the night before. Getting downwind of the wrong caddie had been known to cost a player a vital shot or two in a tournament.

Usually a player's caddie was selected at the whim of the caddie-master, who called him out by name, handed him a ticket for the day (redeemable later from the caddie-master for £1) and sent him to the first tee. It was during the next few hours that a caddie's relationship with a player would be cemented in mutual respect or torn apart by mutual dislike.

Caddie-master at Fulwell, Harry Honeyman, brother of the boxer Mike Honeyman, allocating caddies for *The Daily Sketch* Tournament

'A lot of the caddies in the old days were, for want of a better word, nomads,' recalls Aitchison. 'They were tinkers, really. A raincoat, sometimes tied with a bit of string, and a cap was the uniform. Yeah, there used to be a lot of caddies you wouldn't want to associate with because there was an element that came just to earn the drink money. There was a bunch of guys who used to sleep rough all the time. They'd herd together in the trees, build a fire, have a few gargles and fall asleep.

'Then there were the characters. Guys like 'Little Mac' who used to caddie for Dai Rees who regularly had to bail him out of jail. He was a smashing guy was Mac but his problem was that when he had a few drinks he'd always pick on the biggest guy in the pub for a fight and he'd often end up inside. Or there was 'Mad Mac' who worked for Max Faulkner. He used to pick up feathers during a round and stick them in his hair. He was mad enough. I once saw him throw a piano player off his stool in a bar, rip the back off the piano, reassemble it and then sit down and play like an angel. None of us had a clue he could play at all.'

It was out of this maelstrom of human flotsam and jetsam that Aitchison forged one of the outstanding careers. Throughout the fifties and sixties he sharpened his skills as well as his dress sense.

'Let's see…Player, Trevino, Lema, Nagle, Irwin, Watson, Palmer, Norman, Torrance, Montgomerie. How's that for starters?'

'Golf was taking off in a big way; it was opening out to the public at large via television. I recognised early on that we caddies had to change, too. We had to look the part and to behave like professionals. I could see that soon there would be no room for the old-style travelling man. The whole game was going through the revolution and we had to be part of it.'

Steadily, Aitchison made his reputation as this revolution took place around him. By 1961 he had picked up Michael Bonallack's bag for The Amateur Championship at Turnberry. They won. Bonallack is now Secretary of the Royal & Ancient Golf Club of St Andrews – his office atop the clubhouse there possessing one of the most coveted views in the world, overlooking as it does the Old Course itself. In all, he and Aitchison won five Amateur titles and though his caddie now says that he was never that impressive to watch, he swiftly adds that Bonallack was one of the very best players you could ever wish to see. Regular golfers will know exactly what he means.

Aitchison was involved in his sixth Amateur Championship victory when he caddied for Trevor Hamer in 1974 at Muirfield but his most public glory days were at The Open Championship. At Hoylake in 1967 he partnered Argentina's Roberto de Vicenzo to one of the most popular wins of all time, and a few years later he was at Lee Trevino's side when 'Tex-Mex' won at Birkdale in 1971 and successfully defended the following year at Muirfield.

Perhaps because each man had risen out of and away from humble beginnings, the American superstar and the Scottish caddie formed not just a professional partnership but a personal friendship that exists still. A glance through Aitchison's employers over the years is a glance through golf's *Who's Who*, a personal honours board that includes some of the greatest players ever to swing a club.

'I've maybe not had them all but I've had most at one time or another,' he smiles. 'Let's see … Gary Player, Lee Trevino, Tony Lema [who was to die in a plane crash in 1966, aged thirty-two], Kel Nagle, Hale Irwin, Tom Watson, Arnold Palmer, Greg Norman, Sam

Torrance, Colin Montgomerie. How's that for starters?'

Still a fit and impeccable figure, Willie is official caddie-master to the PGA European Tour and the Open Championship; still a respected figure even to the young men who now caddie in a very different world. Whereas Aitchison and his pals worked for shillings in their early days and not that many pounds at their peak, the professional caddie as the millennium approaches can make a fortune. Top-line caddies like Alister McLean (Colin Montgomerie), Fanny Sunesson (Nick Faldo) and Philip Molby (Ian Woosnam) expect to earn six-figure salaries from their percentages of their masters' prize-money and, increasingly, their own endorsements. They drive smart cars, live in impressive houses and radiate success. It is all a far cry from the old men in the belted raincoats who dossed down in the woods each evening, and one of the men they have to thank for their elevation is Willie Aitchison.

'There's no comparison, really. On the European Tour the caddies now have their own association with its own badge. If someone does not behave correctly then they can lose that badge. It's a different world and a better one, although sometimes I see a young caddie make a big cheque and immediately think he knows it all, and I think back to the days when a caddie did not have yardage charts or pin placements handed to him on a plate, of the days when you had to know where the wind came from, and when and how it affected a shot, and you had to go out there and eyeball a shot and then tell your player what club he needed. That's a real caddie, but I suppose I would think that, wouldn't I?'

Left: Phil Molby ('Wobbly'), Ian Woosnam's caddie, raking a bunker at the 1996 Masters

Nick Faldo and his caddie Fanny Sunesson

Inset: Colin Montgomerie and caddie Alister McLean, not yet throwing in the towel!

Bill Hopkins wears the look of a man who has spent the great majority of his life outside. His face is deeply lined, his hands large as is likely with someone whose trade has been as a bricklayer. He smokes constantly, coughs nervously. He says he was told to stop smoking ten years ago or else he would be dead within two. 'By my reckoning that means I've been dead eight years already,' he laughs. Nervously, of course.

Born in 1929, Hopkins still lives within a couple of miles of his birthplace in Sunningdale, where the borders of Surrey and Berkshire play with each other's affections. This is quintessential Home Counties land, a haphazard collection of villages and hamlets set amidst soft, southern English countryside. John Betjeman often strolled here, the better to lift his poet's soul after a week spent in London forty miles away. Here you can still hear church bells on a warm summer's evening. Here, you feel, there always will be honey still for tea.

As ever with a caddie, however, Hopkins' main concern throughout his working life has been to have *anything* to set on the table for tea. The need to earn took him as a youngster to Sunningdale Golf Club. Again, as ever, it was a family tradition.

'My dad was a jobbing brickie as well but he used to earn some extra cash working as a caddie down at the club. The members there have always been well off and able to afford to hire someone else to carry their clubs,' he says.

'Dad sorted me out as a caddie. I went down to the club as a twelve-year-old boy in 1941 for my first job and I've been caddying down there ever since. That first day, I caddied for a couple of American visitors and I found the bag I was carrying so heavy I was almost crying by the time we'd completed thirteen holes. One of the Americans asked me what the matter was and I said, "It is too heavy for me, sir". He was obviously a kind man so he immediately said that he had had enough anyway and we walked in. He gave me half a crown instead of the usual 1s 6d. I kept a bob [1s or 5p] for myself and gave the rest to my mum.'

That may or may not have meant honey for tea on the table that night but it did mean that the young Hopkins was able to nip across the common on the way home and purchase his first cigarettes. 'Five Woodbine they were,' he said. 'Cost me 6d [2½p] I think.' It was the beginning of a lifelong addiction to both nicotine and to Sunningdale Golf Club.

The club in Ridgemount Road just off the busy A30 dates back to 1901. Designed by Willie Park and Harry S. Colt (who also designed Wentworth just a couple of miles further along the A30), it is rooted in 'old money'. This is where the men who used to run the British Empire came to relax. The empire may no longer be there to run but the membership as we approach the millennium is still largely composed of the 'right sort of chaps'.

Thus tradition at a place like Sunningdale is important, a jealously guarded commodity in a swiftly changing world. Hopkins has always known this. He has never conceded that any member, or guest, is his superior but he happily admits that when he is working as a caddie he is the employee.

'You have to know your place, to acknowledge that you are there to do a job of work, to assist your player and to make his or her day more enjoyable. Mutual respect is the key and after all the thousands of rounds I've completed down there, I can recall very few problems with anyone not treating me right. I didn't feel

The gypsies of golf

I think.' It was the beginning
and to Sunningdale Golf Club.'

like a second-class citizen, certainly never felt they were better than me. I was just a working man and very, very few people treated us badly, although that Kerry Packer could be a little bit abrupt at times.

'In the old days it was a lot more formal, stricter than it is now. In them days everyone was to be called 'sir' and we had to wear a collar and tie. If you turned up improperly dressed and the caddie-master [Jimmy Sheridan] saw you he'd say, "Get out of my house or I'll lay my hand about you!" And he'd mean it. The caddies used to have to stand around the corner from the clubhouse behind a holly hedge. Jimmy would call you out for a job. Usually he'd say, "Which of you fellows fancies a quick gallop around the Old Course?" This meant a single round on the Old. But usually you'd find yourself toiling away with a fourball on the New Course which is a lot harder to walk.'

The rules back then were simple enough. As a caddie, Hopkins did not speak to his player unless spoken to. His job was to carry the clubs, to suggest yardages and the best line once on the putting green. When he first started he also had to build a tee from sand for his player.

'There were no tee pegs to place your ball on in those days. Instead there was a bucket of sand on every tee and we caddies had to build a little mound of it for our player. The old back used to suffer towards the end, I can tell you. Then when you got back in after a round you would never receive a penny until the clubs had been cleaned. The caddie-master used to do the paying. The caddie would have a ticket and he would exchange this for the cash once the caddie-master was happy those clubs had been done up proper and that there had been no complaints about your behaviour on the course.'

This fee has varied greatly over the years. At one time the caddie was paid the equivalent to a green fee but as it will cost you around £90 to play the Old Course now, that simple arrangement has long since changed, with £25 to £30 the usual amount charged. There have been times, however, when Hopkins has been tempted to tell that day's employer exactly what he thought of his inability to find the deeper recesses of his pocket.

Inevitably, given the location of Sunningdale and its reputation, Hopkins has worked for some rather

Bing Crosby with Mel Smith

famous people. Fame, wealth and generosity do not always go together, however, as the caddie found when he met Bing Crosby one morning at the club.

'I caddied for Crosby several times and always found him a very hard man to work for. He had a reputation for being mean and I found it well deserved. I'll give you an example... One day in 1973 I saw him at the club and he asked me to caddie for him. I'd already arranged a round so I said I couldn't. He was getting his clubs out of his car at the time and he noticed he had not brought any practice balls with him. Now Crosby was a very good player and he never went out to play without practising properly first. I told him I had a bucket of balls I could lend him and that's what I did. When I got back in from my round I asked the caddie-master if Mr Crosby had left anything for me. He said, yes, and handed me back the balls. I asked if he had left anything else but he said no, not a shilling, not a thank you. Now he was a tight old sod.

'But a lot of the old characters have gone. Guys like "Snowball", "Quack-Quack", "Tin-Tack" and "Sailor" were real characters.'

'Lord Lucan, on the other hand, was a great fella. I used to caddie a lot for Charles Benson ['Scout' of *The Daily Express* at the time] and he was big buddies with Lord Lucan. The pair of them used to play a lot with a chap called Maxwell Scott who had so much money it wasn't true. I'd see Mr Scott open the boot of his car and there'd be cash everywhere, it was daft really. The three of them were always playing for a lot of money and Mr Scott would be a pigeon. They used to turn him over something rotten. But no matter what he did you couldn't dislike Lord Lucan. He really was a smashing bloke. Everyone thought so. Mind you, what he was like at home I don't know.

'His regular caddie was a bloke called 'Irish' Martin and he did really well off him. In the days when we were caddying for two quid, 'Irish' would get a fiver off his lordship. Good days those were. There's always been a lot of gambling going on at Sunningdale, some of it real big money too. Everyone knows about it. It's not unusual for guys to play for £200 units and there could be a lot of units in a match. Some of them I've known play for £500 units.

'Of course, us caddies would sometimes have a few bob on our man as well just to keep an interest. But the biggest money we'd make was if our player won a lot, then we'd get a better than usual tip on top of the agreed fee.'

The 'Halfway House' at Sunningdale is a charming wooden shed which makes a fist of pretending to be a café. It also possesses what is probably the finest panoramic view of any eating place in the Home Counties. Here the golfers may pause for some fortified soup perhaps, a sausage sandwich and a drink. It is relatively cheap, well presented and homely.

These days caddies have their own section where they too can order what they wish. For years, however, when Bill Hopkins was caddying he and his colleagues were made less than welcome at this famed institution.

'We always had to go and stand at the rear and all we were allowed, no matter what the weather was like, was an arrowroot biscuit and a ginger beer. Eventually some kind soul also put up a bit of plastic roofing so that when it was pouring down at least the biscuit didn't get too soggy.

'It's all changed now, and for the better in many ways. But a lot of the old characters have gone. Guys like "Snowball", "Quack-Quack", "Tin-Tack" and "Sailor" were real characters. "Sailor", for example, was a dirty bugger – you didn't want to get downwind of him too often. But he used to make me laugh. Every putt was straight according to him – even off the side of a hill. At the end of a long day we all used to meet up in the caddie-shack and usually we'd play cards, often till close to midnight. I'd often lose everything I'd earned that day. Regular, that happened.

'I remember once I went down there on Christmas Eve with £7 in my pocket in the days when seven quid was real money. I lost the lot at cards so I sold my bike for £7, called in at Sunninghill Working Men's Club on the way home and lost all but 30s [£1.50p] at dice. I got home just before midnight with no bike and only 30 bob to last through Christmas. There was a bit of a barney at home that night.

'There's nothing like that now, really. Most of the caddies down there are about twenty years old. In the summer they don't make a bad living but most of them are only waiting to get out and caddie for some big name on the European pro circuit. They are not really interested in being a proper club caddie. They think I'm a daft old sod, I suppose, but I still have my regulars, nice chaps who ring up to book me in advance. They know that I know how to do the job proper.

'Y'see, I love the game of golf. It's an intelligent game as well as a difficult one. I like caddying and I love playing. I play down on the Ladies Course at Sunningdale. Best official handicap I've had there is four which I suppose would be about eight or nine on the big course. Us caddies used to be able to play on the Old Course when it got late on but then some secretary came in and banned us, said it was a piece of sacred land and not for the likes of us. Pity that. But then in ten years' time I reckon proper club caddies like myself will be a thing of the past anyway. You can see the change happening now. Used to be that the majority of members took a caddy out with them but now a lot have got these powered buggies. No, I'm afraid I think we're a dying breed...'

And Bill Hopkins coughs. Nervously.

Left: Eddie Polland, Brian Barnes and Nick Job at Sunningdale's Halfway House, probably the finest unpublicised eaterie in Surrey

Watson and Fyles at the 1977 Open

Suffolk Road, Birkdale is an unlikely place to figure in the legend and folklore of golf. An ordinary little street with just twenty-eight ticky-tacky little houses has been home for the last 100 years to working-class Lancastrians. What Suffolk Road has, however, that no modern planner could provide is one of the greatest backyards in the world.

It is called Royal Birkdale and, with its hills and hollows, wind and sun, this backyard can lay claim to being one of the finest links courses on this sporting earth. But in the hungry 1930s Birkdale was seen by the wee lads growing up in Suffolk Road not so much as a wonderful fusion of God's and man's art but as a chance to earn some cash. A day spent humping a gentleman's bag meant an extra loaf by suppertime. Eventually this was to mean also that Suffolk Road was able to lay claim to a significant share in no fewer than eight Open Championship victories. Jacky Leigh caddied twice for Peter Thomson when he won the Open. Teddy Dalsall guided Johnny Miller to victory and Albert Fyles won with Tom Weiskopf. Overshadowing each of these caddies is Albert's brother Alfie who has known the buzz of walking to the last green and certain victory four times.

His first taste of this sweetest of wines came with Gary Player at Carnoustie in 1968 but it was with Tom Watson that Fyles himself was able to reach out to touch greatness. Three times – Carnoustie 1975, Turnberry 1977 and Muirfield 1980 – Fyles has coaxed and cursed his American master towards victory. The most significant win for Alf, and probably for caddies everywhere, came in 1975.

'I've had some great moments but that win with Tom gave me the greatest professional satisfaction because he had never played golf over here before, never been in the country, so it was a hell of a challenge. Any chance we had of winning seemed to go by the board completely when Tom arrived too late to fit in even one practice round.'

Instead of feeling his way around Carnoustie for a couple of days, Watson had to turn to Fyles and say: 'Alf, I'm gonna have to lean on you this week. Hard.' And he did. Fyles' reaction meanwhile provided the most eloquent response to those critics who suspect a

caddie's role is akin to that performed by a porter.

'Tom not only asked me the yardage on every shot and where the best place to put the ball was, he asked me what club he should take. The man is a genius at the game but I've no doubt that a good 55 per cent of that Open win was down to me,' he says with obvious and justifiable pride.

Yet this partnership of English caddie and American superstar almost ended right there on the final Saturday at Carnoustie. The trouble was the money Watson paid Fyles that week. There simply was not enough of it.

'I thought he was a bit mean and so the following year I worked for Gary Player again,' says Fyles. That was in 1976, the year Miller won by six strokes from Jack Nicklaus and a young Spaniard called Ballesteros. Watson missed the halfway cut.

'I got a Christmas card and several letters from Tom before the next Open at Turnberry but I knew my worth and I was not going to budge,' says Fyles. 'Actually it was Tom's lovely wife Linda who got us back together again. She asked me to have a word with Tom and when she smiles I can't refuse her anything.'

Watson and Alfie talked, a new deal was struck and the caddie took a giant stride into the fabric of the game's history, for it was at Turnberry that the greatest head-to-head duel ever in an Open Championship was unveiled. On one side Watson, on the other Jack Nicklaus. After two rounds they were level. In the third they each shot 65. It was golf and competition of the

most sublime sort, the rest of that glittering field spreadeagled behind the two Americans as though the pair were playing a separate event. Few at the time dared hope that the final round could be anything but an anticlimax and, as he hauled Watson's bag across his shoulder on that last day, Fyles felt the same.

'After I came in from the third round I said to friends that I'd just been part of the greatest golf you could ever see and that there was no way they could repeat that. But they did; Saturday they were just as good. I've never seen a crowd get so excited. In fact at the 9th tee Tom and Jack sat down and told officials they wouldn't carry on unless the galleries behaved themselves. The crucial point for us came at the 15th hole where Nicklaus was fourteen feet away while Tom was off the green and a long way away. When Tom's chip rolled in for a birdie I saw Nicklaus rock back on his heels as though he'd been slapped in the face. He knew then that this Open was not his.'

It almost was not Fyles' Open either, for before he was to reach the 18th green the stocky little man with the rattling laugh was to be trampled beneath the feet of a mob of over-excited fans. The incident left Alfie with a permanent memento of this Open victory – the only one he has, as caddies are not thought by the R&A to be worthy of a keepsake.

'Someone stamped on my right wrist so hard they ground my watch right into the skin. I've got the scar and the lump to this day but it's a small price to have paid because at one point I feared for my life out there.'

So the 'daft job' that started for Fyles when, as an eight-year-old boy, he used to hurry from his paper round to caddy at Birkdale for 9d a round and 3d off the caddie-master, ended in glory.

'It is a daft job. Not many people would like to do it. It's hard work y'know. Aye, in the old days we often had to bed down under a hedge behind a green some-where. We used to call it "staying with Mrs Greenfield". If you wanted a wash you just stopped at the first pond. It's better nowadays, of course, but back then we were still living a gypsy life. There was just always something in my blood that made me want to be a travelling man.'

n for a birdie I saw Nicklaus rock back on his heels as though he'd been slapped in the face. He knew then that this Open was not his.'

Chapter 3: 'I say, you there!' (The Club Secretary…or the Art of Handling Members)

'Most golf club secretaries need to be as thick-skinned as a rhinoceros. Unfortunately quite a few also seem to be dinosaurs.'

Anon

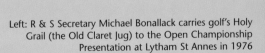

Left: R & S Secretary Michael Bonallack carries golf's Holy Grail (the Old Claret Jug) to the Open Championship Presentation at Lytham St Annes in 1976

Right: The Artisans' Championship at Wentworth, 1950. Bricklayer, Mr J Webb and his two young caddies, sons Tony (aged 3) and Roger (aged 5)

The Club Secretary

As this book was being written Launceston Golf Club in Cornwall was advertising for a new secretary: the job description was as follows:

'The successful applicant will be responsible for managing all aspects of the club's business and activities in accordance with the policies and directions of the Committee. Applicants must be experienced in Golf Club administration, computer literate, good communicators with sound commercial and financial acumen, have a good knowledge of golf and possess excellent man-management abilities.'

In other words the Launceston club was looking for what in effect was a managing director of a small but not insignificant private company. This is a recent phenomenon. For much of the twentieth century the golf club secretary in Britain was a rather clichéd figure. Invariably ex-military, usually to be found with moustache rather than without (women, of course, were rarer than a hole-in-one on a par five), the secretary was more often than not a conservative chap, recently retired and willing to work for little financial return.

'Doyle-Davidson…is admittedly ex-military but I suspect he has always been willing to march to the beat of a different drummer if he believed the rhythm was moving him in the right direction.'

In place of money, many secretaries enjoyed the power they could radiate in their small kingdoms. Some were happy to be no more than executive lackeys to the various committees that really ruled the club but others used their personalities and experience of command in the Services to impose their will on members. These men wore tweeds, spoke brusquely and preferred an egg-stained tie to a cashmere sweater in the club bar. They were traditionalists, and golf clubs, with their dislike of change and their love of a hierarchical structure, suited these secretaries admirably. The change in both their status and their method of working began to creep in towards the end of the 1960s. Much of that decade's various revolutions had not touched golf clubs, indeed some are still not completely certain who or what The Beatles were, but by 1970 a small trickle of change began to flow unsteadily into some clubs. One man destined to help turn this trickle into an unstoppable flow was Richard Doyle-Davidson.

Born in East Molesey, Surrey in 1927, Doyle-Davidson seems at first glance to be a classic establishment figure, the sort of chap who can wear a checked shirt with a contrasting tie under a double-breasted blazer and yet still look the part. Doyle-Davidson's dress and accent, however, disguise a rather radical figure and certainly a man totally without any of the inherent snobbery that used to afflict so many of his fellow club secretaries. He is admittedly ex-military but I suspect he has always been willing to march to the beat of a different drummer if he believed the rhythm was moving him in the right direction. Richard joined the army in 1944 with the hope of becoming a regular when World War II ended. It soon proved a forlorn hope.

'During the war a regiment had eight or nine battalions but afterwards it only had one so a lot of men had to go and I was one of them. Instead of staying on in the army I returned to London and secured a post with British and International Addressing which was a direct mail and advertising company. I became production director and when I wasn't working, rugby was my passion. Golf I didn't care about at all.'

It was while playing rugby in the London suburbs that he spotted a red flag flying nearby. It intrigued him so much that after the match he wandered across the road to investigate. This is how he first found Richmond Golf Club. By then he had discovered that his rather cavalier approach to rugby meant he was spending an increasing amount of time in various casualty departments. 'This was more than just irritating, it meant also that my playing days were probably drawing to a close. But I loved sport and adored competition so I decided that golf was to become my thing.'

Right: Richard Doyle-Davidson revitalised Wentworth when he joined the club in the 1970s. This view, taken from the TV hoist during the World Matchplay Championship in 1989, shows the 18th

A perfect English setting at Brancepath Golf Club

Typically, he entered into this new game with commitment as well as enthusiasm and soon became a more than decent player. This combination of a rugby injury, the red flag on a green at Richmond and his job with British and International Addressing was to lead, circuitously admittedly, to Doyle-Davidson becoming one of the best-known, and certainly pioneering, club secretaries ever.

Nothing, however, was further from his mind when in the mid-sixties his company invited him to set up a new operation in Sunderland, employing 500 people. It was a small adventure and Doyle-Davidson, by now married to Barbara, moved with typical enthusiasm into a new home in Sedgefield and joined Brancepath Castle Golf Club where he continued to nurture his four handicap. His future seemed secure. Certainly, having discovered how much he liked the north-east, he har-boured no desire to move south again and expected his life to revolve simply enough around his family, his work and his golf club until retirement. Life, however, is never more unpredictable than when everything seems perfectly settled. Several years after his move north Doyle-Davidson was struck by the sort of mid-life crisis that has become all too familiar in Britain over the last decade. Instead of yomping gently towards retirement he found himself made redundant when his firm was taken over by a larger American company and the Sunderland operation was closed down. Down-sizing had arrived and Richard was one of the first victims.

'I remember sending off more than fifty letters for jobs and not even getting a reply. It was a bad time. Sunderland, even then, had two and a half times the average national unemployment. There I was at forty with a wife, one child, another on the way, and no job. And apparently not much hope of a job.'

It was then that Harold Macmillan came to the res-cue – or at least gave Sunderland's latest unemploy-ment statistic an idea. 'I don't remember why I heard a particular speech by the ex-Prime Minister but I do know that he said, "There are 300,000 people unem-ployed at present and inflation is at two and a half per cent. Enjoy these things because you will never have

but it was terribly run-down, really. In some parts there were five layers one on top of the other, while paper was peeling off the walls in places.'

created a House Committee and a Social Committee which allowed them some say. They still didn't have power but they did have influence.'

Doyle-Davidson, meanwhile, had power. In the early eighties Greg Norman discovered this when he turned up unexpectedly with three friends to play the West Course. By then the Australian was established as one of the world's leading players, and as several of his titles had been won at Wentworth he considered the club a sort of second home.

Unfortunately, on this particular day it was also home to several hundred other men practising for the forthcoming English Amateur Championship, and the West Course was closed to everyone but these enthusiastic competitors. Doyle-Davidson had to walk on to the first tee and tell Norman that he could not play.

Despite his affable and apologetic approach, Norman took the news badly. 'He couldn't believe I would not allow him to play and really got very upset and angry. Finally he stormed away, saying he was going to play Sunningdale. I rushed inside to ring the secretary there and warn him Norman was on his way. Before I was able to ask him not to allow Norman on there either he told me that their course too was busy. A journalist found out about the story and wrote an amusing piece about it. I, of course, was depicted as the archetypal, crusty old secretary who had thrown this famous golfer out of his club. I photocopied the story and sent it up to Muirfield where Paddy Hamner was secretary and a few days later I received a reply. It simply said: "Congratulations, Richard, you've finally made it as a secretary!" '

'No matter who you were, if Hamner did not like the cut of your jib then you did not play Muirfield.'

Twenty years ago I drove from St Andrews to play golf at the Crail Golf Society at Balcomie, a wonderful eighteenth-century links on the northernmost corner of the East Neuk in Fife. We had not booked ahead, preferring to arrive shortly before 7am on a glorious summer's morning. The Balcomie clubhouse was locked but we knocked anyway. After a few minutes a sash window above our heads was thrown open and the secretary appeared, his face covered in shaving foam, his vest gleaming in the sunshine, while a pair of very practical braces dangled round his waist.

'Sorry to bother you,' I said. 'We wondered if we might have a round and how much we need to pay.' The secretary looked down and said, 'Away you go and play. You can come in and see me when you've finished.'

Not all secretaries are so accommodating. For some of these men the golf club is a substitute for a personal kingdom, a territory they rule with a rod of iron. The undisputed champion of the despotic secretaries was a gentleman called Paddy Hamner who for years ran the Honourable Company of Edinburgh Golfers, otherwise known as Muirfield and a club that fairly reeked of the Scottish Establishment and especially the legal profession. Hamner was by nature irascible and his proudest

boast was that no title or reputation ever impressed him. No matter who you were, if Hamner did not like the cut of your jib then you did not play Muirfield.

The story goes that this former naval captain was approached once by a tall, well-spoken man who inquired if he might play the course that day as he was passing on his way south. Hamner looked at him and asked what school the man had been to. Eton, came the reply. University? Oxford. Were you in the services ever? Brigade of Guards, sir. And your handicap? Scratch at present. 'Very well, you may play nine holes,' harrumphed Hamner before stomping back into the clubhouse.

While I cannot vouchsafe this particular story's accuracy there is no doubt that Hamner's finest hour occurred shortly after Tom Watson won the third of his five Opens there in 1980. The American celebrated that evening with his friend Ben Crenshaw and it is safe to assume that a few drinks were taken before Crenshaw wondered aloud how they all might have performed that week if they had been playing with hickory-shafted clubs and guttie balls. When someone appeared with just this equipment Watson and Crenshaw strode back out on to the course to play a few holes accompanied for some reason by a piper. This was to prove their undoing.

While they played the 18th, Hamner was having supper at his home adjoining the first fairway. It had, as usual, been a long week and the secretary was tired. He was also astounded when he heard the sound of bagpipes wafting across his dinner-table. Intrigued, he set off to investigate.

Whether the new Open champion Watson saw him coming or not is unclear but there is no doubt that the American scarpered swiftly back to his hotel. Crenshaw, meanwhile, was so absorbed in his putting that he did not hear Hamner's approach until the master of Muirfield bellowed at him, 'Crenshaw, what on earth do you think you are doing. You have no right to be on this golf-course. See me in my office in the morning.' Crenshaw's protests that he had to leave early to catch a flight apparently made little impression on Hamner as he strode angrily back to what remained of supper.

Overleaf: Tom Watson on his way to winning his third Open at Muirfield in 1980

Left: The salary's OK but the job is worth it for the view alone
– Michael Bonallack's office balcony at St Andrews

Right: One day his prince did come. Prince Andrew and
Michael Bonallack study form

As Secretary of the Royal and Ancient Golf Club of St Andrews, Sir Michael Francis Bonallack OBE understandably believes he may have the best job in the world. This, of course, is open to debate, some of us suspecting that the backstage dresser at the Folies Bergère might just have the edge, but what is beyond question is that Bonallack has the best office on this sporting earth.

Situated atop the R&A clubhouse in Fife, Bonallack sips morning tea while gazing out over the Old Course. From his veranda in the evening he can switch to a pink gin while peering through his telescope at the latest victims playing the world's most famous stretch of golfing real estate. Downing Street or the White House may have their own certain cachet but, aesthetically at least, Bonallack has Tony Blair and Bill Clinton four holes down with four to play. Except during the week of The Open Championship when Bonallack's domain is a dusty Portakabin somewhere near the 18th green. From this place he lords it over the oldest and probably the greatest championship in golf, his benign, understated exterior disguising an eagle eye for detail and a fine appreciation of what The Open should be about.

It was in his temporary office that I spoke with Bonallack during the 1997 Open at Royal Troon on the Ayrshire coast. As he leaned back in his chair I felt that here is a man as well suited to nosing a good wine as *le patron* of any decent restaurant. A brilliant golfer – he won five Amateur Championships between 1961 and 1970 – Bonallack never considered turning professional. 'If I had done so I suspect I would have starved,' he said. 'Back then there was no European Tour. The professional season began in May and lasted just a handful of events. Serious players such as Tony Jacklin had to go to America to earn a good living and apart from perhaps a lack of talent I never really fancied travelling that much.'

Instead he joined a property and investment firm in London, running their leisure division from an office just off Buckingham Palace Road where he set a lifelong trend of only inhabiting places which afforded decent views. In 1983 he was invited to take over the secretaryship of the R&A; it was an offer he could not wait to accept. 'If you have the chance in this life of combining your passion and your profession then you should take it. I am very, very lucky.' As secretary he presides over a group of like-minded men of almost every nationality. The committees are amateur and Bonallack's brief is to encourage professional decisions while jealously guarding golf's traditions and etiquette as well as upholding and updating the laws and promoting the sport.

As most of the committee 'hackers' are also some of the major movers and shakers from the worlds of politics, commerce and the law, this is not too onerous a task – in theory at least. It does, however, demand a man of serious patience who is also a natural diplomat. Bonallack, a small smile constantly playing around his lips, appears to have been born for the role. Of course, his effortlessly patrician air, his blazer and tie, tend to reinforce a stereotypical upper-middle class image. It is a charge Bonallack is happy to meet head on. 'We may look like old fogies – we may indeed even *be* a bunch of old fogies – but we try very hard not to *think* like a bunch of old fogies,' he said. 'Someone wrote in a paper this week that it was a good job we made a decent profit on this Championship because most of it seemed to be being spent by the R&A on gins in the clubhouse. As members of the Championship Committee and other officials are not allowed to drink until after the last putt has dropped on any day of The Open I felt this to be a little unfair.'

It is, in fact, colossally unfair. In 1997 The Open grossed around £14 million. The profits from this, around £6 million, will fund every R&A event from the Seniors' Open to the Boys' Amateur. The R&A are also the main donors to the Golf Foundation – set up to promote golf amongst youngsters – and offer interest-free loans to golf clubs suffering from complaints such as land erosion. Only after this do the chaps buy each other a drink. Things, however, do sometimes go wrong at an Open.

In 1983 Bonallack found himself standing by the sixth green at Royal Birkdale at 3am because it had been vandalised by campaigners who felt a local man had been jailed as a result of a miscarriage of justice.

'It might be just for them to do this but it's unfair on us,' was his quiet summation that morning.

If that Open started with a serious hiccup, it ended with a belly-laugh after the retiring secretary, Keith Mackenzie, had the bright idea of revamping the presentation ceremony, moving it from the 18th green to halfway back down the last fairway.

'Before the Championship we erected a stage and marked the four corners with white spots on the fairway.

As Tom Watson played to the 18th green in the final pairing we had a gang of men hidden behind a sand hill ready to haul out this blessed thing which really was quite huge. As they made their move so did the crowd, ducking under the ropes and running towards the green so they could see the end of the ceremony. The men put the stage in place and Keith was thrilled. But then those spectators at the back of the crowd around the green looked behind them and saw

this thing which hadn't yet had the tables and chairs placed on it. They raced back and hundreds of them climbed on to it so they could see the presentation which they all assumed was going to be on the green as, traditionally, it always had been.'

And indeed this tradition was upheld, the R&A bowing to mob rule. When asked later what the stage had been for, the old and the new secretaries proudly announced that they thought it would be helpful to erect as a spectator platform. Once again the media left an Open wondering at how forward-looking these blazered gentlemen really were. The stage has not been seen since. But then it wasn't really needed, for The Open always has been its own theatre of dreams. Just like Michael Bonallack's office.

The Road Hole on The Old Course at St Andrews in the 1940s: the toughest hole in golf

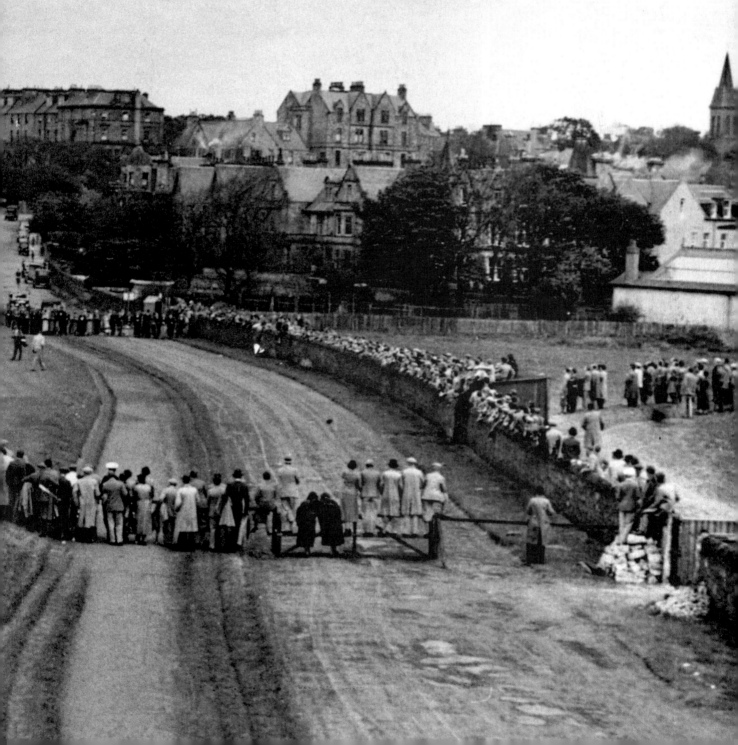

Chapter 4: The workers in the fields

' Some golfers would complain about conditions if they were playing on Dolly Parton's bedspread.'

Jimmy Demaret

Left: Cnut's spirit lives on. The greenkeepers' 'rhythm section' tries to stem the tide at The British Ladies' Championship at Walton Heath in 1968. Play was later abandoned

Right: Seeding the fairways during construction at St George's Hill

The Greenkeeper

Greenkeepers are the great unsung heroes of golf. While a golf course is either a victim or beneficiary of natural location, the actual condition of the course is entirely down to man's ingenuity and his ability to deal with the many and varied enemies that conspire each year to frustrate his efforts to maintain the 120 acres of real estate that make up the average golf club.

Modern irrigation methods, whereby a computer controls the amount of water laid across a course, have removed some of the fears of greenkeepers as they contemplate their greatest enemy, drought, but there are still many foes to be fought. There is always the prospect of disease affecting what can be upwards of forty different varieties of grass on a course, and there is also vandalism, floods, tempests and wild animals to combat. Modern machinery and chemicals may have eased the physical burden slightly for the average greenkeeper but he must still react swiftly to each

'Because of the war the golf course was designated as emergency grazing land as well and there was sheep all over…'

day's challenges, combining the skills of gamekeeper, farmer, forester and horticulturist as he does so. Yet until recently there was little or no formal training. New greenkeepers learned the job from older, more experienced men – a sort of secret society that handed its rules and objectives down to each generation by word of mouth. The men themselves were invariably drawn from rural farming communities, natural inheritors of the benefits of hard work, fresh air and, for the most part, a sort of mastery of your own day.

At the majority of private clubs there is a Greens Committee made up of interested members who oversee the greenkeeper, suggesting and requesting a change here, less grass there, as the seasons roll on in their rhythmical way. Some Greens Committees are good at their job but many do not really have a clue, their duties restricted merely to requesting a second cut on greens shortly before an important competition. This, often, is perhaps as well because greenkeepers are a proud bunch of men who value their knowledge and their instinctive sense of independence.

Cecil George is such a man. Naturally sociable, his warm Scottish burr accentuates the nature of someone you sense has spent the great majority of his time at peace with himself, his surroundings and what he did. Born in Thornliebank, eight miles outside Glasgow, Cecil began working for his uncle, who was a gardener, when he left school in the late 1930s. At this stage it would be wrong to suggest that he had a thirst to become a greenkeeper, but it was certainly a thirst that led him into the job that was to dominate his life.

'I was on a job with my uncle and although it was late summer it was still very warm. I suppose I was going on fifteen years old at the time and just across the road from where we were working was a golf club. I developed a raging thirst and as there was nothing else nearby I walked across the road to the club to see if I could purchase a lemonade or its like. I got the lemonade okay and while I was drinking it a chap from the club asked me what I was doing. I told him I was working nearby with my uncle but that I'd be looking for some other work soon as the gardening stuff dried up in the winter. He asked me if I'd be interested in greenkeeping as they were looking for a young lad, and that's how the whole thing started for me.

'There was, of course, no apprenticeship. I just learned from the head greenkeeper as best I could. When I first started I had two jobs. First, I was in charge of raking the bunkers and making sure they were in good order, and second, I was in charge of the sheep. Or at least bits of them. Because of the war the golf course was designated as emergency grazing land as well and there was sheep all over Whitecraigs Golf Club at that time. My job was to follow them around with a shovel and gather up all the sheep shite into a bucket so the members didn't have to walk in the stuff. It was not a great job. When the members talked about S.S.S., they meant Standard Scratch Score but to us greenkeepers S.S.S. meant Sheep Shite Shovel.'

Because Whitecraigs was a relatively prestigious

Douglas Pate and Col John Rees, head greenkeeper and secretary respectively at Birkdale during The Open in July 1962. They decided that as the underground water level was so near to the surface, a suction pipe inserted into the earth, would enable water to be pumped out to deliver water to the dry fairways

and well-off club there were six greenkeepers in total, roughly double the average number. But if the course was to be kept in good order this was just enough men. Explained Cecil, 'By the time I started, the last horse had just gone but all we had by way of replacement was a couple of little tractors and a motorised mower that kept breaking down. Basically only the fairways were machine cut; everything else was cut by hand and it was a painstaking business to do it properly. When I started I was paid 10 shillings [50p] a week and I lost 1s 6d out of that to various insurances.

'It had to be a job you did out of love because there was precious little reason to do it otherwise in those days. In Scotland we were just regarded as labourers and we were looked down on. The only people beneath us were the chaps who emptied the dustbins but there wasn't much in it if you see what I mean. Certainly our working conditions were terrible, just awful. We, however, just accepted it all because that was what we expected and that was the way it had always been. We were never, ever allowed into the clubhouse, of course. Instead we used to go to our lit-

tle shed and sit around in there during our breaks. There was no toilet, no running water. Nothing.

'The clubmaster would bring us the occasional pot of tea but that was about it. It was all still very much a forelock-tugging type of thing back then. But, you know, greenkeepers were – still are – very friendly people and their companionship made up for a lot. We all used to love the job and that was the main thing. It's changed a lot nowadays, of course. It's a living wage for a start and that helps. As the years went by, I became secretary of the west section of the Scottish Greenkeepers' Association and I went to agricultural college and learned formally about fertilisers and different types of soils. I felt this was an obvious good thing and tried my best to promote the idea that young men coming into the job should learn these things properly. Now there is a proper emphasis on education

A 'Sisis' turf aerator coupled to the Ransomes 'Overgreen' with which Gordon Child was familiar

Right: Gordon Child winning his local club Championship at Calne in 1948

Below: The Lancashire Golf Team pictured in the early 1950s when Gordon (back row right) was a member

whisky during the war and an old rubber apron. Charlie was intrigued. "What are these for?" he asked. We still had the sheep grazing at that time so I saw my chance. I told him that he would have to use the corks to bung up the arses of the sheep while we were away for the weekend. He turned a bit green but managed to ask, "So what is the apron for?" I told him that when he returned on Monday mornings he had to put on the apron and go and take the corks out. Charlie, I recall, was not impressed.'

Around the time Cecil George was establishing his reputation as a bit of a joker, Gordon Child, too, was learning the art of greenkeeping. Unlike Cecil, however, Child had always suspected that this was to be his job. Born near Ilkley in West Yorkshire in 1931, his father and grandfather had been greenkeepers and it was perfectly natural that he, too, moved into the trade under his grandfather's sharp eye at a Sheffield club. There

and the whole greenkeeping scene has been lifted onto a higher plane.'

This, of course, has been a necessity. There is much more golf played as we approach the millennium than there was forty or fifty years ago when the game was almost exclusively middle-class as well as middle-aged. Now commercial considerations demand sophisticated greenkeeping if a course is to survive the traffic its fairways endure throughout the summer months, and the increasing demands of the environmentalists have meant greenkeepers having to pay attention to the protection and encouragement of plants and animals. Long gone, for example, are the days when worms would be injected with strychnine before being hurled down mole holes to kill off the burrowing animals which can blight a course as well as threaten a greenkeeper's sanity.

Although Cecil had his share of bad moments he never lost his instinctive urge to have a laugh when the opportunity presented itself. 'When the weather turned really bad at Whitecraigs we used to fill in our time by clearing out the sheds which were always getting into a dreadful state. I was doing this one day with a new lad called Charlie who was, as you'd expect, a bit green around the ears. Suddenly, in a corner we came across a bag of old corks that I knew had been used for bottling

would be injected with strychnine before being hurled
course as well as threaten a greenkeeper's sanity.

was, however, a moment when Gordon was tempted to break the mould and find his way as a professional golfer instead. Certainly he was a talented player and by the age of sixteen he was off scratch. One of his friends, however, counselled against the move. Neil Coles, one of the best players of his generation (and now the chairman of the PGA European Tour) told Gordon that there were 'only half a dozen of us making a decent living out of tournament golf so think carefully before taking the plunge'.

It was good, if harsh, advice and Gordon decided to take it. 'My other alternative I suppose was to become a club professional but I preferred the thought of greenkeeping. I still played golf, of course, and had a long spell at scratch and plus-one, playing at county level and even managing to play in a couple of Open Championships. As a greenkeeper I couldn't play on any of the courses I actually worked on but I became a member of another club and that's where I played.'

Ironically, Gordon played most of his county golf for Lancashire after moving to Royal Birkdale, Southport, famed site of many Open Championships. Before then, however, he had to learn his first skill as a greenkeeper deep in the heart of Yorkshire at the Dore & Totley club just south of Sheffield.

'My first job was finding out how to put plates on the club horse. He was called Prince and I suppose he must have been very nearly the last of his line. Prince was used to mow the rough and I'd sit behind him on a metal seat which juddered and shook so that when you stepped off the blessed thing you knew you'd been at work.

'I remember us getting the first motorised mowers, which the old boys weren't keen on, although if they'd been sitting behind Prince like me they might have been a bit keener. Anyway, that was the start of the modernisation and the beginning of courses becoming much more manicured. It was a very different kind of scene back then. There was much less golf played on a course so that we hardly saw a golfer in the mornings and very few more in the afternoons. The local shopkeepers would turn up on a Wednesday afternoon because that was half-day closing for them but most golfers played in the summer evenings. It was all very relaxed, really.'

And when they did play, they played more quickly than today – a source of much aggravation to Gordon. 'It was very unusual for anyone to take more than three hours. Crikey, even in the quite high-level amateur competitions that I used to play in we rarely took more than three hours. Now they seem to copy the professionals, studying their putts for ages and not being ready to play when it's their turn. The expectation now is that it takes more than four hours, which is daft really.' But if this is a source of regret, some of the other changes receive Gordon's applause – working conditions for a start.

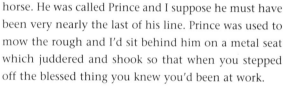

While at Moor Park Gordon received a visit from leading US
agronomist Jim Beard (far right)

'It was unheard of for a greenkeeper to go anywhere
near the clubhouse. Instead we went into work early in
the morning, went to the old shed to get our gear and
work out what we were doing and then, when lunch-
time came, we'd eat our sandwiches in the same shed,
sitting on some old cans. There were no facilities for
washing either so if you'd been working with a fertiliser or whatever, tough. Golf clubs generally were one of
the last parts of British society to see any need for
things like health and safety or treating their workers
with respect. Now greenkeepers are much more edu-
cated people and many, like myself, have been made
honorary members of the club they've worked for over
many years. There are still some places, however, that
have yet to catch on to the fact that we're coming up
to the twenty-first century.'

After learning his skills in Yorkshire, Gordon moved
to Birkdale to find out what it was like looking after a
links course with its•different grasses. From there he
joined Blackburn G.C. as Head Greenkeeper before travelling south to St George's Hill in Weybridge, Surrey,
and on to Moor Park in Hertfordshire and ultimately
on to Churston in Devon where he happily 'escaped the
rat race'.

It was while he was at Birkdale, however, that he

'There were no facilities for washin
generally were one c

either so if you'd been working with a fertiliser or whatever, tough. Golf clubs
the last parts of British society to see any need for things like health and safety ...'

Gordon Child on duty at Churston

because it looks better and probably plays better, too. In some respects we're coming full circle. You might think that with all this modernisation there are fewer green-keepers but this is not so. The fact is that so much more golf is now played, there has to be a lot more work carried out on a course if it is not to go to rack and ruin. No, the future is very bright indeed. The only thing that saddens me is the creeping Americanisation of golf in Britain.

'To me, the best courses are still the old, traditional ones. Too many of the new ones are not in step with our tradition. Some of them have such long walks

discovered not everything you find on a golf course is what it seems. 'One of the old boys came in one morning and asked who'd been putting fertiliser down behind the 16th green. "There's a white powder there," he said. "I know it's fertiliser because I licked it and that's what it tastes like." The Head Greenkeeper looked at him and grinned. "It's not fertiliser; you've just licked the old club president, Mr Marsden. His ashes were scattered behind the green last night."'

At the beginning of 1998 Gordon Child became chairman of BIGGA, the British and International Greenkeepers' Association which was formed in 1987 and which bonded together various national associations. It was, naturally, the highlight of this gentle man's career. As with Cecil George, education has been at the core of Child's professional life and he now takes much pleasure from the fact that embryo greenkeepers are faced with an array of full-time diplomas, of National Vocational Qualifications and of Higher National Diploma courses.

There is still, however, a place for the seasoned voice of experience amidst all this academia. 'Nothing gives me more of a thrill than seeing one of my lads take up a top job somewhere and it's also nice that the older guys like myself are still asked for advice. Proper education is paramount and we now have that but there still remains a vital role for experience to play.

'Now we have all manner of machines capable of doing many of the jobs quicker than we ever could. But more and more clubs want their greens hand-mowed

take up a top job somewhere and it's
like myself are still asked for advice.'

between greens and tees that you almost need the help
of a local guide to make the journey. Then there are the
greens with their huge humps and hollows that look as
though a herd of elephants have been buried underneath them. It's all alien to my eye. It's all fine in its
own way but it somehow just doesn't seem to fit in
here. My idea of a great golf course is somewhere that
if you left it to nature for a few years it would blend
back into the countryside swiftly so you would never
know it had been there in the first place. The great
architects took a piece of land and worked with it; they
didn't dig it up and start again.'

Gordon's team at Churston

Carling World Golf Championship, Royal Birkdale, September
1966. View of the 13th with Bruce Devlin putting in the final
round watched by Peter Butler

Chapter 5: Why did women ever want to play the game?

'Call every woman "Sugar" and you cannot go far wrong.'

Walter Hagen

Left: An officer and a lady in 1941. Henry Cotton carries his wife's clubs while 'Toots' contemplates smiling...but changes her mind

Women in the Sport

Sometimes I wonder why women bother at all with the game of golf. This, I hasten to add, is not the raving of a rampant misogynist: it is just that the female sex historically has been made so unwelcome. This, though regrettable, was at least understandable in the first half of the twentieth century when the belief that women – cuddly, pretty, little things that they were – were simply were not in the same sporting class as men.

Indeed, they were seen as second class in almost every endeavour. Good lord, they were not even astute enough to deserve the right of a vote in our democratic society until they started throwing themselves underneath horses and chaining themselves to railings. Things have improved, of course, but there is still a serious undercurrent of resentment thriving in

Golfing ladies at Torquay golf club 1903

too many golf clubs. In far too many of these dusty establishments women are endured rather than (politically correctly) embraced. There are still too many 'Men Only' bars, too much restriction placed on when they may play. Saturday mornings are often held back for men because it is still suspected by the dinosaurs who run some clubs that 'the little woman can play during the week when her only other duty is to ensure her husband's supper is on the table when he returns from work'.

To be fair, many of the women who do join clubs do their sex no favours. There still exists a not insignificant number of middle-class ladies who regard feminism as some sort of terrorist organisation determined to outlaw the bra whilst at the same time poking out men's eyes with a sharp stick. At many clubs women pay seriously reduced subscriptions and are happy to

do so even if this means a consequent loss of status. Equally, many of these clubs refuse to allow females to pay the full (male) sub because if they did so then they might also have to be treated as equals. Sad though it may be, sexism and snobbery still march hand in hand down far too many fairways. There are, for example, no women members of the Royal and Ancient Club of St Andrews and there is no acceptable reason why this should be the case. Sooner or later the R&A will have to concede that women should have a role within their organisation that is not defined by either a dust-cloth or a word processor, but the chaps have mounted an impressive rearguard action against such a move. Until recently their explanation for an all-male enclave was that there was no ladies' toilet available. If one then asked them why not, the answer was that there were no lady members. Now this argument may have a pleasing, witty ring to it but it remains evasive and stupid.

Mind you, the defences have been breached in almost every other respect. There are now female club secretaries, female professionals and, in professional golf at least, women who hold executive office. The women's game in America is hugely healthy with the US Women's Tour enjoying high-profile television coverage and sponsorship. In Britain we are still catching up. Women's professional golf did not start on this side of the Atlantic until 1979 and has struggled to thrive ever since, despite producing several world-class players. As I write, the women's pro game appears in a particularly sickly state with sponsors deserting the Tour and TV turning a blind eye to the female game. And this despite a prediction from the highly respected Henley Institute that over the next decade it is women who will provide most of the growth within the game. Some golf clubs may still prefer women to wait silently back home in the kitchen but manufacturers would seem best advised to increase their production of pastel-coloured golf bags.

This influx of women into the game undoubtedly will change golf in many ways and no one will be more

The ladies' putting course at St Andrews circa 1884

delighted to witness their arrival than Marley Harris. Now and then every game throws up a natural, someone blessed by the gods, and Marley was just such a person. She was twenty-two years old, however, before she realised it. Born Marley Baker in Wimbledon in 1928, she enjoyed a privileged, middle-class childhood. Always athletically gifted, she dabbled in the usual school sports but preferred to devote most of her leisure time to dance.

'I adored it, darling, absolutely adored it,' she told me when we spoke at her home in Budleigh Salterton, Devon. Marley says 'darling' a lot. She is that sort of lady. At seventy she remains glamorous and bubbly, her enthusiasm for the game of life apparently undimmed. She insisted on preparing lunch on the day of our interview and, almost inevitably, it was pheasant accompanied by a robust wine. Before this game bird, however, the game Mrs Harris mixed a serious gin and tonic and served up a plate of smoked salmon. This, it transpired, was particularly apposite since it was precisely because of smoked salmon that the finest lady golfer of her generation took up the game.

First, though, she pursued her love of dance, leaving school and becoming a professional dancer good enough to take part in several West End shows and to share the stage with the likes of Arthur Askey in *The Love Rocket*. At twenty-two she married a garage-owner called Spearman and it was as a 'rookie wife' that she made her way to Harrods in 1950.

'I was holding my first ever dinner party, darling, and I wanted some smoked salmon which has always been my favourite. It was while I was waiting in a long queue at Harrods that I noticed a sign on the wall saying, To The Golf School. I'd never played golf but my first husband did and I thought it would be fun to have a go. So I followed the signs and found myself eventually in the golf school where the resident professional asked me what I wanted. In those days one really dressed up to go shopping so I wasn't exactly prepared for golf. I said I wanted to learn the game. He asked me when I wanted to come along and I replied, "Why not now?" He looked a bit taken aback but I just took off my hat, kicked off my shoes and I had my lesson there and then.'

That evening over dinner she told her husband and guests of her modest adventure. They were surprised and a few, inevitably, were patronising. Never one to be patronised, Marley decided she would persevere with this game. Her husband she says was 'quite reasonably set up' so there was never any question of her having to work for a living.

'At that time we lived near Marble Arch so off I trundled to Regent's Park the next morning where I knew there was a golf school with nets near the zoo. I had no clubs or anything so the pro gave me a five iron

Four years after she had first swung a club in Harrods she represented England and before she finished in 1965 she had played in three Curtis Cup sides, represented the Commonwealth and been voted Golfer of the Year by the Association of Golf Writers in their prestigious annual poll.

and a seven iron to use. He also asked me if I needed a lesson. I told him, "No thank you, darling, I learned yesterday". Can you believe anyone being so naïve?'

Intrigued by this naïve and attractive young woman, the professional watched as she began to hit balls. He was amazed at what he saw. In truth Marley had not yet begun to learn the game but her natural swing was a thing of serious, technical beauty. 'After a while he came over and said that if I was being honest about never having played before, I could be a champion golfer; indeed that if I applied myself, then within three years I'd play for England. I was astonished. I didn't know what was good or bad but I did know that I enjoyed hitting a ball.'

Within six weeks Marley had joined her husband's club, Sudbury, and her first three cards of 101–103–105 gave her a handicap of 35. Armed with this modest handicap she immediately entered 'The Captain's Day' competition which was a stableford and which she promptly won with the outrageous score of 56 points. Here, clearly, was a star in the making. Her opponents, however, did not celebrate this stellar arrival in their midst. Instead, quite a few of these older, tweedy women yelped 'cheat'. Marley was shocked that anyone could think such a thing. Despite the fact that her partner supported her claim that her round was faultlessly honest, she did not receive the prize due to her. Her handicap, however, was cut to 19 immediately. It was at this point that a lesser spirit might have given up the game prematurely but when Marley told her husband what had happened he advised her to 'go and practise and then tear through them like a dose of salts'. Marley decided this was the way to go. Unwittingly, those unsporting and older ladies at Sudbury G. C. had played their mean-spirited part in the creation of an outstanding golfer.

Given her circumstances Marley might easily have become one of those ladies-who-lunched. Instead she became a woman obsessed with practice. Over the next two years her handicap dropped to just four and she won everything on offer at Sudbury. No one ever again accused her of cheating. Equally, few wanted to play her in any competition.

'I was neither popular nor unpopular at the club. Certainly I hope I was modest because I think the great thing about golf is that it is such a terrific leveller. The fact is that you've never quite got it taped and the more I played the more I realised this truth. This was also the reason why I practised so much which I suppose was unusual in those days.'

Inevitably, the more she practised the better she got. Until she got too good! At least as far as some of the Sudbury ladies were concerned she did. This sad fact struck her forcefully when she turned up at the club one day to pay her shilling to enter the monthly medal competition. 'I'd just handed over my 'bob' and signed my name when I overheard two women say, "If she is playing, we are not". I was appalled. I remember thinking, "Oh God, this is the pits". I did not play again in any club competition. Not ever.'

Instead she began to practice even harder, turning the garage at home into her own practice area complete with nets so she could continue to sharpen her skills through the winter months. It was an extraordinary commitment by this extraordinary woman. And it paid off spectacularly. Between 1955 and 1965 Marley won the Middlesex Ladies Championship a staggering eight times. Clearly she did not need to enter a monthly medal! Her record during the ten years she competed at the highest amateur level is astonishing by any standards. She won the British Ladies twice, the English Ladies once, the Sunningdale Foursomes, the Roehampton Gold Cup and the Hovis Ladies, as well as a bouquet of other glittering trophies. Four years after she had first swung a club in Harrods she represented England and before she finished in 1965 she had played in three Curtis Cup sides, represented the Commonwealth and been voted Golfer of the Year by the Association of Golf Writers in their prestigious annual poll.

Not surprisingly, she was offered the chance to turn professional. She did not hesitate before turning it down. 'One of the big manufacturers wanted me to turn pro in 1964 but in no way did I want to do that. Really the only women professionals there had been by then were Jean Donaald and Jesse Valentine and,

Right: Postcard from 1914. Why should men encourage women to play golf?

without being unkind, they were no more than high-profile reps for Slazenger and Dunlop. There was no professional women's circuit in Britain or Europe so if you wanted to make a living you had to go to America and that was something I really did not want to do, darling. I loved the amateur game and, to be honest, I didn't need the money. I don't want that to sound wrong but that was the fact. Golf back then was a very exclusive game. It was marvellous for those of us who were in it and really it never struck any of us that it was unfair that so many people were kept out of the sport. It was just the way it was in those days and one didn't question it, just as we ladies did not question the fact that we were never expected to go out and get a job. Different times, darling, different times. Life was gentler, at least for us it was, although I know that other people were having a hard time. But just everything appeared so much sweeter than it is today when it all seems want-want-want and everything seems to me to be harder and uglier.'

For Marley everything in life seems to have been in a particularly soft focus. At seventy she remains positive and bubbly, her good looks peering through the inevitable marks of ageing. Forty years ago she was regarded as a sensation, appearing regularly in the William Hickey gossip column in *The Daily Express* and even having a wax model made of her by Madame Tussaud's for 'ordinary people' to gawp at. She brought an energy, a skill and a sexiness to a game that had been seriously dowdy before her arrival. From the start she had upset as many people as she had delighted by wearing crisp, smart clothes on the course.

'I never saw that it was necessary to dress down for golf. I like to look pretty smart all the time so why should I be any different on the golf course? Others, however, seemed to prefer gardening clothes. It wasn't my way and, although it wasn't designed to, it got me noticed.'

She was in fact just part of a natural, feminine progression. Just as Mo Connelly outraged Wimbledon by wearing gold-coloured knickers on the Centre Court, so Marley took women's golf on to a different plateau

as far as sporting fashion was concerned. Right from the moment Gladys Ravenscroft sent Edwardian society into a swoon by rolling up her sleeves while playing in the 1909 Ladies Championship at Royal Birkdale, the battle for the sporting rights of women has been engaged. But as Marley dressed up so the dressing-downs increased. Suddenly she became increasingly aware that women walked a tightrope and that men, and some women, were only too ready to shake that rope.

'I chose not to wear baggy skirts all the time. I wore feminine stuff. The newspapers used to call me "Queen of the Links". One chap even wrote, after one match for England, that I'd played particularly well that day and put the headline on his article, "Windmill Girl Saves England". It was a bit embarrassing but mostly it was just a hoot, darling. I mean I'd never been near the Windmill Theatre (where young women used to undress on stage) but the fact that I'd once been a professional dancer was enough and once the Windmill tag was introduced it continued to appear no matter how many times I denied it. I suppose it was too good an angle for the reporters to ignore. They were all divine people, those pressmen, but some of them could be a bit naughty. I suppose one of my proudest claims is that I once knocked Christine Keeler off the front pages in Australia at the height of the Profumo scandal. I was playing for the Commonwealth at the time and I wore a pair of tapered silk trousers one day. A full-length picture appeared in the Sydney papers the next day. I suppose they thought it was a bit sexy for a golfer. I just thought it was quite good.'

It was while in Australia that Marley came up against her biggest case of sexism. Until then her talent and her privilege had protected her from most of the nonsense that went on daily in golf clubs.

'I really hadn't noticed much anti-women stuff. Oh, I'd once walked innocently through the main doors at Hoylake only for an usher to jump up and shout, "Madam, madam" and take me straight back outside so I could enter via the ladies' staircase at the side. I thought that was a bit silly. But in Australia,

Right: Marley Harris has an agonising look on her face as she makes a mess of a putt on the 17th green, when partnering Mrs Michael Bonallack, in the Avia Foursomes at the Berkshire Golf Club, in 1971

despite the fact that we were the Commonwealth team, we were told that we would have to enter all the big clubs like Royal Sydney and Royal Melbourne by side stairs. I told them it was nonsense and refused to do it. If I was playing golf, I was going through the main doors. But then so much about Australia was silly in those days. We were invited to endless cocktail parties which always had the men standing at one end of the room and us at the other. I just thought it was so parochial. I remember the place we were staying in Sydney was being decorated while we there. It was disgusting, paint and ladders and mess all over the place. And it was freezing. So much so that we had to send out for extra blankets and hot water bottles so we could make it through the night, darling. The Australians didn't care. The men's team was following us out in six weeks' time and all they cared about was getting the place tickety-boo for the chaps. It really was the pits. I loathed Australia then. I'm sure it has all changed now but back then I didn't know how the Australian women put up with it.'

Then, as suddenly as she had begun to play the game that had made her famous, Marley stopped playing. It was as though a giant full stop had been dropped into her life. There was no lingering farewell: for Marley it was just goodbye.

'I'd had enough, darling. For five years I was basically No. 1 in Britain which meant I led every English and British team. That was a lot of condensed pressure. I'd always wanted to stop when I was at the top and that was what I did. I never saw the attraction in hanging on until inevitably I became a tail-end Charlie. Now I look back and I am so glad that I did it all. It was such fun. A lot of it was girlie nonsense perhaps but we enjoyed it so. My time may have had its faults but I wouldn't exchange it for today. I look at the Women's Tour and I don't see that they are any better than us. Certainly they don't dress any better. Laura Davies is out on a limb as by far the best woman golfer we've ever produced but I don't think the rest are any better than, say, Angela Bonallack or Barbara McIntyre. Now, would you mind passing the biccies, sweetie...' Marley Baker-Spearman-Harris – never a

Windmill girl, but always, effortlessly, a genuine star.

Liz Kahn, too, is a star in her own way, which is to say different to anyone else. Liz is an outstanding journalist but she is also a character, a genuine, at least slightly eccentric, and bohemian woman who for most of her life has marched to the beat of her own drum. She also learned to play golf in the fifties, and came from a comfortably well-off class. Money, you suspect, has never been a problem for Liz but bias and unfairness have always made her bridle.

'It was natural for me to play golf as a child because my mother was captain of Chorleywood Golf Club while my grandmother played at Harewood Downs. As a little girl I used to go along to the common and just bash a ball around with a club and I suppose I was around fifteen by the time I actually joined my mother's club. It all seemed very friendly and very nice. I suppose the women I played with were all reasonably genteel ladies and I never noticed any sort of anti-women thing. One didn't, back then. I think the only time my mother ever really experienced true independence was during the war when she went into the Women's Voluntary Service. Until then she'd always had staff in the house. My father, meanwhile, didn't like golf much. He was a Cambridge blue at rugby and he also played cricket. Those were his sports. I was a bit of a tomboy growing up. I don't remember much playing with girls: it always seemed to be boys. Of course, when I joined Chorleywood I tended to play with girls but that was a natural thing to do.'

While Liz was never to become more than a competent golfer, her contribution to the game has been twofold. First, her writing helped spread the gospel but second, and more importantly, her determination to improve the lot of women within the game has had a significant effect. First, though, Liz Kahn had to become a journalist. Initially this had not been a burning ambition.

'My first job was working for a chap in the City who was a member of The Not Forgotten Society which was made up of disabled ex-servicemen. I ended up on the switchboard. Then, and don't ask me

cocktail parties which always had the
I just thought it was so parochial.'

Above: The Kahn swing seen at the tender age of fifteen on Chorleywood Common

how, I went to California where I got a job with some stockbrokers. Don't forget this was the sixties, everything was free and easy, and employment of some kind was pretty easy to come by. Then I got a job at a second-hand car sales place. I got the sack from that when I began giving out news bulletins in a very English accent over the Tannoy to relieve the boredom. Eventually I ended up working for a doctor in Beverley Hills and then I came home and got married. Then, accidentally, I got into journalism. I became friends with a sportswriter called John Ballantine and he took me along with him to Wimbledon when he reported there, to give him a hand. I loved it but I couldn't envisage being a tennis writer because that would have meant spending too much time in the USA and I'd just got married. So my brief flirtation with journalism came to a halt.'

Soon afterwards Liz argued with a friend who claimed that most people in England knew who Arnold Palmer was. Intrigued by the discussion Liz carried out a 'vox pop' in the street and discovered that of the 120 people whom she approached, only one-third had heard of the great American golfer. She won her bet. More significantly she re-ignited her writing career. 'I thought it was a good piece to write about and to my delight and surprise I found a magazine willing to use it. On the back of that I started writing for *The Daily Telegraph* and *Golf World* magazine. It wasn't always easy. The first time I wrote for *The Telegraph* was from an event at Wentworth and when I went on to check if everything was okay the sub-editor who was dealing with my copy that evening rather sternly asked me what I was doing, trying to be funny in my article, and that *The Telegraph* was a serious paper. I just laughed and asked him what he meant by *trying* to be funny?'

By now, Liz was a reasonably established writer about golf and so her friend Ballantine and her new friend Peter Dobereiner (for many years the adored golf correspondent of *The Guardian* and *The Observer* newspapers) proposed her for membership of the Association of Golf Writers. This was new territory, for there had never been a female member of the AGW,

and Liz's application for membership was rejected much to Ballantine's and Dobereiner's chagrin.

'I suppose I was the only woman writing about golf. Enid Wilson and Elizabeth Price used to do some but I was into it full-time. I was very disappointed at the AGW's attitude which I suspected was based on the fact that I was a woman although they denied it. The then secretary, Ron Heager, told me he was sorry about it and that he would write me a letter asking for me to be admitted to clubhouses. Armed with this I would duly approach various security people at clubhouses and the like, show them my note – and promptly be thrown out. Unknown to me, Mr Heager was going behind my back and warning them about this woman who would probably turn up and claim to be a bona fide journalist. It was very upsetting actually. Then one day I spotted one of those boards that contain cardboard facsimiles of official badges, amongst which was the blue and white AGW badge. I sweet-talked the commissionaire and asked him if I could have it as a souvenir at the end of the event. He agreed and I used this cardboard badge for many years to get where I wanted.

'I thought it was all a bit of a hoot, really. I wasn't very feminist in those days although I recognised the bias and thought it regrettable. But on the plus side I had a nucleus of players who looked after me, guys like David Talbot, Lionel Platts and Hedley Muscroft, for example. They kept me going. I never had any problem getting interviews and so I specialised for a while on feature writing. I also did trade pieces and travel articles and then I wrote a book about Tony Jacklin which was well received and which obviously helped my reputation. It didn't help me join the Press Golfing Society, however. I applied but I was told that as they played at courses where women didn't play, I couldn't join. I was kept out for seven years in that manner.'

In fact Liz eventually did join the PGS and went on to become their first female captain in the early

nineties. In 1979 she also was accepted by the Association of Golf Writers. By now she was making regular trips to the United States to cover the growing women's tour over there. She had already met some of the major female American stars.

'To be frank I found them all a bit intimidating at first but I soon realised that they were in fact very independent and achieving women. I was impressed. It was like discovering a new world in a way. I began reading feminist writers, everyone from Simone de Beauvoir to Germaine Greer. Then when *The Independent* was launched I began writing about women and golf and the inherent problems of sexism in the game. It was all so silly. I'd known about it, suffered from it, for years but now I wanted to take it on and challenge the *status quo*. It seemed that women were being treated more equally everywhere but that golf was stuck in a time-warp.

'I remember once, for example, when I went to play at Little Aston near Birmingham, which is a beautiful place but where the attitudes used to be rooted in stone. I was sitting on a bench outside the clubhouse waiting for my male partner when I was asked to move despite there being no one else there. I was told the problem was that the bench was placed outside a window and that if any of the (male) members cared to look out, they could see me. I ask you! Actually I don't think that at that time a woman could even drive into the car-park to pick up her husband after a game. But they weren't alone in their attitudes. Not by a long way. I was always having problems at St Andrews with the R&A who never have had a woman member, which is absolutely appalling. I walked into their lovely clubhouse one day, unchallenged, and on into a huge room where I was looking at the pictures on the wall, when a man I hadn't noticed – he was sitting in one of those big chairs – suddenly turned around and said, "Excuse me but women are not allowed in here, but don't worry, I can't see you". I thought that was rather nice so I carried on looking at the pictures and then a waitress came in and threw me out. Sometimes we just can't win.'

Liz's problems with the Royal and Ancient did not end there. She was determined as a journalist to obtain the same access as her male colleagues to locker-rooms and thus the players. To this end she wrote before one event to the R&A's deputy secretary, George Wilson. To her delight he agreed she could enter. Unfortunately it appears that Mr Wilson forgot to tell anyone else about his decision and her coup.

'I wanted to take it on and challenge the *status quo*. It seemed that women were being treated more equally everywhere but that golf was stuck in some sort of time-warp.'

'He said to me that I could go into the locker-room because I was only doing my job, so in I went only to be ejected bodily. I was shocked. For two years I 'phoned and wrote to the R&A arguing the case. At one stage lawyers from the National Union of Journalists advised me that if I went to court then we would win. But I felt that it was better if we continued to talk and so that's what I did. Now we women can enter the locker-rooms at the various championships. In my experience the players don't mind and it is just common sense. Mind you, the R&A were not alone. For years the European Tour would not allow women in. Indeed, although they may tell you differently, as far as I'm concerned they still don't.

'So it is changing, but only slowly. My generation of women have been the victims of conditioning as have the men. I think we have all missed out on things we should have enjoyed. Not just in golf, in life. The game has merely mirrored what has been going on around it and sometimes the women have been their own worst enemies. But now there is a new generation of women who are not willing to put up with the nonsense. The older generation of men is naturally dying out but I fear it will still be an awfully long time yet before the game of golf treats women as it should. At least it is on the right track. It's about time.'

1800 TU

Chapter 6: 'Trust me, I'm your manager'

'My manager just got me to do commercials for a mattress company and I fulfilled a life's ambition. I'll get paid for lying down.'

Lee Trevino

Left: Lee Trevino leaves no-one in Lancashire in any doubt that he is a Texan. He posed for this shot at the Alcan Tournament at Royal Birkdale in 1968

Right: Derek Pillage (centre) with Gay Brewer (left) and Billy Casper

The Manager

It is difficult to the point of impossible for today's professional sportsman to imagine life without a manager to hold his hand – usually when guiding this hand towards a contract for clothing, equipment or to represent a company otherwise unrelated to sport. As sportsmen have become the new rock-'n'-roll stars, distant yet glamorous and aspirational figures to their legions of fans who for the most part worship them via television, so the opportunities to cash in on success away from the field of play have escalated.

In golf these opportunities are manifest to the point where world-class players like Greg Norman and Tiger Woods can command far more money just to *play* in an event than they will earn if they actually *win* that week. Of course, they must win regularly if they are to remain towards the peak of the commercial mountain but the very fact that they are being paid, sometimes as much as $250,000 to play, gives these men a huge advantage over the rest of the field, making it far easier for them to go for the risky shot that might bring victory than the ordinary professional, who is worried about paying his mortgage and keeping shoes on the children's feet. 'Try playing for money when you haven't got any,' American pro Lloyd Mangrum once observed, and it is a very fair point.

While managers or agents were not unknown in golf forty or even fifty years ago they were still a rarity. Certainly outside the world of pro golf itself they were anonymous figures. This changed when Mark McCormack first met Arnold Palmer in the 1950s. McCormack, a lawyer, was already a keen golfer and like everyone else at that time he was bowled over by Palmer's cavalry charges through the US Tour. Palmer, of course, is the player credited with creating the massive public interest that in turn has led to today's sophisticated and money-laden golf circuits. It was not just a matter of Palmer being a thrilling golfer; the ex-marine was also the sport's first working-class hero, an 'Ordinary Joe' who could do extraordinary things on a golf course but who never lost his ability to stay in genuine touch with the public.

McCormack recognised immediately that here was a perfect marketing vehicle for some of America's biggest companies. He offered to handle Palmer's business affairs and the two men shook hands on a gentlemen's deal that, it is claimed, has never been formalised since with a contract. So successful has McCormack been in marketing his first client that Palmer, despite now being in his late sixties, remains one of America's most potent sporting symbols and is still one of the very highest annual earners from sport-related sponsorships and endorsements. McCormack, meanwhile, has gone on to establish the No. 1 personal management company in the world. This very clever lawyer has also completed the circle by creating original sports events in which his clients may compete and win money, out of which he takes a percentage. It is perfect synergy.

In Britain, the manager was slower to arrive but now there are many men and women who earn their living from sport without ever having to hit a ball or withstand a right hook or a tackle themselves. Among the first to identify properly the potential for extracurricular money available to a successful golfer was Derrick Pillage. This former sailor and amateur boxer managed the first significant stable of British players and in so doing set new standards for what was possible for a decent professional to earn. When he began, however, Pillage had no intention of becoming a manager and before he could begin to ponder exactly what it was he wanted to do with his life he had to find his way back to England. This, for a man born in Plymouth, was not as easy as you might have thought.

Top left: No part of a golfer's body is out of bounds. Greg Norman advertises Reebok

Left: Mark McCormack at the event he created, The World MatchPlay at Wentworth

Right: 'Swoosh' goes forty million dollars. Tiger Woods advertising Nike

'I soon became known as the "blue-eyed Mexican", which at least meant I stood out when we were all looking for a bag to carry.'

Born in 1930, Pillage never knew his real parents. Instead he was adopted by a sailor and his wife. While still a very young boy, however, Pillage's life was turned upside-down once again when his father decided that a war with Germany was inevitable. 'He was being posted out to China somewhere in the navy and he felt that I needed to be moved to somewhere safer, so he arranged for me to go to my mum's sister.' This lady, however, lived in California and so Pillage was bundled up, a name tag placed around his neck, and was sent by boat to New York. 'There I was put on a train by a porter, and a lady looked after me on my way to Salt Lake City where another porter handed me on to a couple of strangers who accompanied me to Los Angeles, where I linked up with my uncle and aunt who lived in Santa Anna down near the Mexican border.'

This Mexican link was to prove significant to Pillage many years later when he became manager to one of golf's true superstars, but before this he had a new way of life and a radically different environment to absorb. Instead of the grey English climate he found a land of sunshine and oranges and, of course, all-year-round golf which in turn provided him and other youngsters with the opportunity to earn twenty-five cents a bag as caddies at the local club.

'Most of my friends were Mexican and with the tan I always had I soon became known as the "blue-eyed Mexican", which at least meant I stood out a bit when we were all looking for a bag to carry. It was a wonderful childhood, for my uncle was a club pro and my auntie was a keen player, so golf was soon an important part of my life. Of course, I played a great deal as well as caddying so that by the time my pals and I were fourteen, we were all off scratch or one handicap. Then in 1947 I returned to England to be reunited with my adoptive parents. It didn't work out, however, and I was pretty miserable. The fact was that I didn't know Mum and Dad any longer and I couldn't stand the climate. In fact I ended up suffering pleurisy. No wonder I was desperate to go back to America.'

During his National Service (despite his initial dislike of Britain he swiftly worked out that eighteen months in the Royal Navy was a better deal than the four years he would need to serve in the National Guard if he returned immediately to the USA), Pillage mostly developed his boxing skills. After this he made it back to California where he played golf and made his way eventually into the public relations world. However, while his career was going well, his golf suddenly and dramatically took a turn for the worse.

'When I was twenty-four years old I was out playing a bunker shot. It was a difficult shot with my ball up against the face of the bunker so I had to stand with one leg on the bank. I thrashed at the ball and fell over. Ordinarily all this would have caused was a bit of embarrassment on my part but on this day I fell in a funny way and I broke my back. It was a bad break. Bad enough to mean I had to spend the next two years in a wheelchair, the experts telling me that I'd never walk properly again. But I was determined that I would. I just refused to give in. I started walking with the aid of sticks but I still needed that wheelchair part of the time for several years. Golf, naturally, was out of the question. It seemed that that part of my life had come to an end.'

By the mid-1960s, however, Pillage felt confident enough to take his first, hesitant, steps back on to a golf course again. By then he was in public relations for Warner Brothers, and playing golf again was not only relaxing but a very useful part of the working environment for someone involved in the film industry. He joined the prestigious Los Angeles Country Club and it was here that the next phase of his professional life was to be forged.

'I'd met a guy called Tony Grubb who was the British PGA Champion around that time and when he came over to California I fixed up a game because he was trying to pre-qualify for the Los Angeles Open at my club. He introduced me to a young lad he had over with him. This was Malcolm Gregson who was the Assistants' Champion at the time and I could see straightaway that here was a player with genuine potential. He didn't have a manager, of course, so Grego became my first client. He had a contract with the Scottish club-makers Ben Sayers so I went to North Berwick to the company's offices with him to negotiate a new deal.

'As chance had it Ben Sayers had just appointed a

Left: Derek Pillage playing against Harry Weetman who is looking on stoically in the background

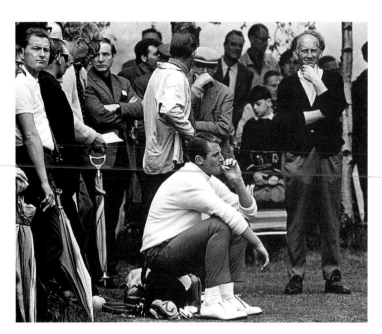

Brian Barnes looking supercool during the Agfacolour
Tournament in1969 at Stoke Poges. He won the tournament, his
first win in Great Britain

Top right: A more mature Barnes throws a playful punch at
European Tour Official George O'Grady during the presentation
of the Martini International at Wentworth in 1980

new managing director at the time who had never done
a player contract before. Neither had I, of course, but
when he asked me what I thought a good figure for
Malcolm would be I suggested £5,000. I then held my
breath because I knew the best contract in Britain at
that time was around £1,000 for Neil Coles. He said
that was fine so I decided to push it and asked about
bonuses for winning or finishing in the top three. I got
£250 for a win plus a percentage for finishing second or
third. I then got him to write into the contract that
while Malcolm obviously would play with Ben Sayers
clubs he could choose whatever clubs he wanted for his
driver, his wedge and his putter. Then I negotiated
more bonuses for Ryder Cup and World Cup appear-
ances. Malcolm just sat there saying nothing, his eyes
getting bigger and bigger as the deal went on. I asked
him eventually if he had anything to say and he said,
"Yes, what about if I win the Harry Vardon Trophy?"
The Vardon Trophy is awarded each year to the leading
professional at the end of the season. I got him another
fifty quid for that.'

This was quite sensational stuff at the time and
within days the news of Pillage's ability to broker a

mouthwatering deal was doing the rounds. The first
player to respond was Scotland's Brian Barnes who had
been a school chum of Gregson's at Millfield.

'Barnesy rang me and became my second client. He
was also my longest, still with me when I decided to
retire from the management game in the late 1980s. In
fact Brian refused to accept that I had quit and it was a
good two years before he finally believed that I had
gone. Funnily enough, I never had a contract with
Brian – he was with me seventeen years and we never
had a contract. Extraordinary really. After that the players came in thick and fast. They were all young guys
naturally, players like Nick Job and Bernard Gallacher,
and I did some outrageous things with some of them.
Barnesy, for example, had played for England at Youth
level but his parents were Scottish and I told him he
should elect to play for Scotland when he turned professional because he would get into things like the
World Cup so much easier. Three weeks after he
declared himself to be Scottish, his dad wrote to *Golf
Illustrated* complaining. I had to laugh.

'I then managed to get a guy called Craig Defoy
declared Welsh despite his having been born in
America. In truth I got away with murder. Probably my
best coup was with Sandy Lyle. By the time I'd signed
him, Sandy had played already for England at Boys,
Youth and full international level but his parents were
Scottish and his name, Alexander Walter Barr Lyle, certainly was Scottish so Sandy became a Scottish hero. It
was all a bit outrageous but in those days you just had
a few drinks with the right people and it was sorted out.
Now it would be much more difficult.'

Taking on a posse of young professionals soon
turned out to be rather more complicated than Pillage
had hoped. They were, for example, not the most
worldly-wise bunch of chaps he had met and Pillage
had to be not just a business adviser but a father-figure
as well. 'They were so naïve back then, some of them
anyway, that I even had to teach them about sex.'

While they all seemed able to absorb this particular
lesson fairly easily, a few continued to have trouble
adjusting to the money they were earning. Principal
amongst this group was Lyle. The gentle young Scot

players like Nick Job and Bernard Gallacher,
ome outrageous things with some of them.'

was a golfing natural but he was also a naturally laid-back character who assumed at the beginning of each day that life would never do anything other than treat him well. Golf certainly treated him well. Although Lyle has struggled over the last decade, his first ten years as a professional saw him reach up to touch the game's highest peaks with victories in The Open and the US Masters and a gilt-edged collection of other titles from around the world. All this time the money was rolling in but initially Lyle seemed rather non-plussed as to what to do with it.

The first alarm bell rang for Pillage when he took a telephone call from Lyle's bank manager at his then home town of Shrewsbury. The banker told a startled Pillage that he was a bit embarrassed to call but that he felt Mr Lyle's financial adviser should know that there were many thousands of pounds lying in Sandy's current account and thus earning no interest. No sooner had Pillage sorted out this error than he discovered that not all of Sandy's money was going into an account of any kind.

'We were flying to the United States together, and Sandy was fiddling around with his flight-bag at some point in the journey, when he asked if I'd like a Mars bar. I said I would and so he started to empty out the contents of the bag to find one for me. I just sat there open-mouthed as all this currency began to emerge. There were dollars, lire, francs, sterling traveller's cheques – you name it and it was there. I picked it up and sorted it out and it came to over £3,000; and this was in the days when that really was a lot of money. I asked him what on earth he was doing carrying that sort of money around and he told me sheepishly that I had advised him always to make sure he had some cash on him. I had to laugh. Oh, and he had a dozen Mars bars in there as well.

'He is a smashing guy but he often did daft things when he was younger. One of his best was when he won the European Open, and at the prize-giving he was handed an envelope which was said to have his cheque inside. Sandy never opened it. Instead he ripped it up soon afterwards believing it to be empty. It wasn't and I had to write to the organisers to ask for another

cheque please. They took a bit of convincing that Sandy had ripped up their original one.

'But that's how it was back then. Everyone was on a learning curve as golf took off and the money involved became bigger and bigger. It was the same with appearance money. All the main players were on appearance fees of some kind or another. Sometimes it would be money, sometimes I'd negotiate an airline deal or a hotel deal instead. And there were other ways in which a star player could be guaranteed to turn up at your tournament as well, for often a sponsor would be told that so-and-so would play for a certain amount of money but only if the sponsor looked after some other players from the manager's stable.

'Looking back it was a lot of fun, and probably the most fun I had was on the African circuit where we all used to start our year's work and where the welcome was fantastic. Nowadays the pros play in America or Australia or the Far East in the first few months of the season, but back then the European Tour did not start

The Golfing Lions (l to r standing) Malcolm Gregson, Sandy Lyle, Brian Barnes, Carl Mason; (sitting) Golfing Lions captain Tommy Horton, manager Pillage and Sam Torrance

> ...the greatest star Pillage ever looked after was a man who admits that if he had not become one of the greatest golfers ever to draw either breath or a three iron, he might well have ended up in prison instead.

until mid-April and although the Safari Tour was a little bit ramshackle at times, if you wanted to earn some money in February or March that is where you went. Sometimes the cheques failed to make it out of the country you were in for a while and sometimes the local tax turned out to be pretty hefty but the one guarantee we all had was that the players were guaranteed competitive golf and everyone else had a fabulous time.'

While Lyle turned out to be the biggest British star for Pillage – eventually he sold his contract to the McCormack agency – this extraordinary character managed some of the most fondly remembered names in British golf in his prime. These included the likes of Carl Mason, Ewen Murray, David Chillas, Guy Hunt, Tommy Horton, Sam Torrance and David Ingram. But while this is an impressive cast list, the greatest star Pillage ever looked after was a man who admits that if he had not become one of the greatest golfers ever to draw either breath or a three iron, he might well have ended up in prison instead. When Pillage was known as 'the blue-eyed Mexican', little did the exiled English boy know that one day a brown-eyed Mexican called Lee Trevino was to have a pivotal effect on his life.

'I first saw Lee at the Orange County Open in Anaheim, California, in 1966 and he was dressed all in black except for his red socks. He was telling all and sundry that he had to play with pick-up golf balls as he couldn't afford new ones, so my first impression was of a rather brash young Mexican. A year later Murray Luxford, Tournament Director of the Bing Crosby Tournament at Cypress Point, asked me if I would go out and play a practice round with two qualifiers – one was a tall, skinny kid called Gerry McGee and the other was a small, stocky youngster called Lee Trevino. We played in heavy drizzle but despite the conditions I was so impressed with the way this young Mexican-American could work the ball that we agreed that when he came to England the following year I would take up managing his affairs outside the USA.

'But what did I really know about the man? I returned to England and wrote an article saying that I had found the next superstar; the way I had written it

'Supermex', with wife Claudia (number one), winning The British Open at Royal Birkdale in 1971

made people think I had done it tongue-in-cheek, especially as I had misinterpreted and therefore misspelt his name as, with his broad Mexican accent, I ended up calling him Leigh Trevano. Not for long, however. That year, he started making his mark by beating Bert Yancey in the US Open, his first professional victory. He had by this time taken on an American manager called Bucky Woy who ended up commissioner for the American Professional Bowling Association.

'Lee had a tattoo on his arm with the name, Ann, his first wife. He was by now married again to a lady called Claudia who, incidentally, has never had the credit she deserves in my opinion for helping Lee get established as a pro. It was Claudia who had scraped together the money somehow to enable Lee to play the US Tour and it was Claudia who looked after his finances, as well as his children, and who tried to keep him on the straight and narrow in the early days.

'Anyway, whenever Lee played golf he covered up his tattoo with a Band Aid plaster and we decided to try to get him an endorsement with Band Aid over the next two years. We failed and from then on "Ann" was shown to the world. About three years later at the same Crosby event an exhibition was set up with Lee, Bert

Left: A young Trevino in the Alcan Tournament at Royal Birkdale, 1968, trying to cover the 'Ann' tattoo with a Band Aid

'Lee's humour was always infectious...'

Yancey, Ron Cerrudo, Sean Connery and myself. We all had officers from the military base at Ford Ord as our caddies. After about three holes I developed the most chronic toothache and it was an amazing coincidence that the man caddying for me happened to be the army dentist. He said that if I filled in all the appropriate forms he would operate on the offending tooth later. I would have signed my will over to him at that moment but we waited until the end of the match before I was carted off to the dentist's surgery while everyone else disappeared. Then an hour later, much relieved, I was taken to the officer's mess and who was sitting there waiting for me but Lee – holding court in his usual inimitable manner with everyone roaring with laughter at his joking about. I asked him what on earth he was doing there and he said, "Waiting for you". That was Trevino. An army-chauffeured car drove us back to our accommodation and I might say a very unsteady Trevino went off to his room.

'Over a period of ten years Trevino must have hired and fired at least twenty people and, of course, that involved me...at least ten times. But I just didn't take any notice and carried on. I knew that the Mexican blood would get very hot on occasions. In the early days the local bar was his favourite training ground, which helped him get rid of some of the pressures. I remember him coming in one night at about 2.30am after a good night partying, when he was due on the first tee at 8 o'clock the next morning. But he teed off on time and went on to equal the course record. I think the change came in his life when he was playing golf one day with Gerry Heard and Bobby Nichols and all three of them were struck by lightning. A paramedic thought Lee was dead at first but eventually he made a full recovery. Typically, his first words when he came round were, "What a harsh penalty for slow play. In future I'm going to carry a strong one iron – even God can't hit that!"

'Lee's humour was always infectious but what really impressed me about him over the years was his dedication to his craft. They talk about the hard-working Faldo and the modern golfer but I don't think any man worked as hard as Lee during his professional career.

'The year he won The Open at Muirfield (1972) he brought over a lot of his friends from El Paso, Texas, to stay with him in a mansion in the village of Yester. The place was full of antiques and came complete with a butler named Nicholas. This mansion, called Yesterhouse, had originally been the home of the Duke of Wellington's daughter and it was full of Napoleonic antiques. For example, there were two Napoleonic snuffboxes of priceless value on the dining room table and Trevino, who was never one to hold back, told the owners to remove them to a place of safety as "the people I have with me steal ashtrays from Holiday Inns". The owner had stressed the value of the items and the furniture adorning the house, and in the Yellow Room he pointed out six Van Dyck paintings and underlined their immense worth. Trevino took several minutes to study them intently and then stood back and said, "I never knew Dick could paint".

'Trevino had come to Muirfield not liking the golf course but, professional that he was, he sent his loyal friend and caddie Willie Aitchison in search of the greenkeeper for advice on how hard the greens would be and also where he thought the pin positions might end up. He then decided that long iron shots would bounce through the greens so he took two small-headed woods, the equivalent to four woods today, and shaved the face back between a modern five and six wood. He also brought over a sandwedge which, instead of having the conventional lines, had punch marks on the face which he believed gave him extra spin. It was a ladies' club and had belonged to a professional called Helen Hicks; in fact her name was inscribed on the back. During the US Open he had shown it to the committee to see if it conformed to regulations; he did the same with the committee in Canada and followed the same procedure with the R&A at Muirfield.

'I was informed after the championship that the chairman of the wrong committee had looked at the club but the R&A said the decision stood that it was not an illegal club, which was something of a relief at the time. Trevino in fact gave the club to me and I then presented it on indefinite loan to the R&A; it hangs in the clubhouse at St Andrews to this day. So if you visit

Trevino with caddie Herman

'These local caddies were always black
Herman, and couldn't see why he was

Lee was a fool not to return to Augusta. He said it didn't suit his game as there was no rough but he could work the ball either way and was a phenomenal putter, plus Augusta was as long as the courses he played on the US Tour when he won all his majors. Of course, he did eventually return to Augusta, many years later, but he was past his prime and I suspect Lee must now regret his decision as he would have been one of the few players to win all four majors if he had been victorious at Augusta.'

Pillage believes that Trevino's brush with death via a lightning strike left a permanent, if invisible, scar on the previously happy-go-lucky Mexican's personality. The old Trevino never really returned. Instead of parties and beers, he became a 'bit of a recluse' for a while. He remarried for the third time (another Claudia – Lee used to joke that it meant he did not have to have the monogrammed bath towels changed) and although he put on a show for the public every time he played, after his round and a practice session he would disappear to his room where he would order room service.

'While Lee changed in some ways after the lightning strike, he stayed just the same in others. In particular his generosity to others never wavered. For example there was a televised golf exhibition at Walton Heath with Lee joining former Open champion Max Faulkner, film star Sean Connery and Formula One legend Jackie Stewart. Lee got to know Max quite well and thought he was a real character, which of course he is. When we went to sign the contracts Lee wanted to know how much Max was getting for his fee. He felt it was not enough, insisted it should be a four-figure sum and that if the sponsors would not agree to this then it was to be deducted from his own cheque. When Max eventually saw his cheque I think it was a shock because it was three times more than he won as The Open champion in 1951.

'I occasionally still bump into Lee at various golf events. He is getting a little grey now and his son is caddying for him on the US Tour but he is still capable of the most fabulous and entertaining golf, even if he claims at times that he can't really compete with what he calls the "flatbellies" or much younger guys on Tour.

those hallowed grounds, go and see the club that holed the shot from the back of the 71st hole to beat the unfortunate Jacklin who ended up three-putting from around 18ft.

'If that was a heartbeat-quickening incident, I would think that my most embarrassing moment with Lee came when we went to Augusta for the US Masters and he fell out with Clifford Roberts, the Augusta supremo, following the death of Bobby Jones. I am not quite sure what caused the rumpus but I believe it was to do with having to use an Augusta caddie.

'These local caddies were always black guys and Trevino wanted to use his own caddie at that time, Herman, and couldn't see why he was not allowed to, as Herman was black as well. Anyway, war was declared between the two of them and the next morning Lee turned up with a trailer-home which he parked in the players' car-park. He never went near the clubhouse to change or anything and he also made a few remarks about Clifford Roberts. One must remember that Augusta is just south of Atlanta which, of course, was burned to the ground by General Sherman during the American Civil War. When Trevino was on the putting green he let it be known to the gallery that he would never return to Augusta but his manager (pointing at me) would be coming back with Sherman. I wanted the ground to swallow me up at the time. In my opinion

His is an amazing story really. I remember him meeting Willie Whitelaw who was then captain of the R&A and Secretary of State for Northern Ireland during the height of all the problems there. Lee engaged him in deep conversation about what was going on in Ireland but I think Whitelaw was trying to set aside the problems, for one day at least, and he asked Lee how he saw his life from his humble start. Trevino replied that if it had not been for golf and the Marine Corps, he would very likely have ended up selling hot dogs on a street corner or maybe even be in prison.

'Instead, there he was chatting with a British Secretary of State. Not bad for an illegitimate Mexican brought up by his grave-digging grandfather in Dallas who used to sneak on to golf courses and get many a clipped ear for it. I don't think we will see the likes of Lee Trevino again. These days all the players seem to come from universities and they all look the same. Trevino made it from the driving range to the Tour but nowadays the pros are whisked away on college scholarships. Not that this is a bad thing but it means that real characters like Lee are harder to find on the Tour.

'How many college graduates, for example, could have taught me the trick Lee did when on the first tee at Pebble Beach in California one day. He said he would give me three shots as long as he could throw the ball twice. I agreed to this and by the 17th hole I was one up with my ball on the green six feet from the hole while Lee's was buried in the rough.

'I thought to myself that this would be when he took his first throw with his ball. And he did. But not with *his* ball...with *mine*! He strolled on to the green, picked up my ball and threw it into the water. Walking on to the 18th tee he said we were all square and he still had one throw left. I was still stunned, of course, and, inevitably, my drive was snap-hooked deep into the Pacific Ocean. Straight-faced, Trevino said, "Just remember I have won one hole up and I still have a throw in hand". It was a harsh lesson but I learned it and I have won a few pounds out of this little game since. There are some things you just can't learn at college.'

Top: Derek Pillage (centre) with among others, Sean Connery, Eric Sykes, Stanley Baker and Graham Hill on another expedition

Above: Trevino holding court with Max Faulkner, Sean Connery, Jackie Stewart and Peter Alliss

Chapter 7:
Writing it like it was...

'I'm sometimes asked why I chose to make my living as a sportswriter and my answer is that it's because the Sports Desk is the Toy Department of journalism.'

America's Red Smith

The Sports Writer

It was during the 1938 Walker Cup match at St Andrews that a small group of sports journalists who specialised in writing about golf decided that there was a need for an association to promote and protect their interests. Since then the Association of Golf Writers has grown into possibly the most respected sports journalists' organisation, representing, and officially negotiating for, golf writers.

The primary function of the association is to enhance where possible the actual working conditions for newspaper men and women. These days this also includes the interests of those working for radio and even web sites and, given the obvious fact that golf is an itinerant sport staged in what effectively is a large field, the AGW fulfils an important function.

Golf has never been the highest profile of sports but the advent of a voracious television audience plus the emergence of genuinely global stars – from Arnold Palmer through Seve Ballesteros to Tiger Woods – has meant a dramatic increase in media attention. There was a time when the British press corps was comprised of just a handful of men. Now the major events like The Open or the Ryder Cup have to employ a full-time secretariat to deal with the many hundreds of requests they receive for journalistic accreditation, and the tent used to house these workers has grown to the size of an aircraft hangar. Some might say that this is a particularly apt analogy as there are so many 'fliers' (suspect stories) written during the major golf weeks.

Whatever the truth of that thought, the fact is that not so many years ago golf writing was perceived as one of the more desirable options open to a journalist, the sport attracting few of the pressures associated with the reporting of, say, football or cricket.

This is not so true today when the PGA European Tour all but circumnavigates planet Earth over a ten-month period and journalists must spend many weary hours travelling hither and thither with not much time to see anything but their hotel and another golf course. There are, however, many compensations, not least of which is the formation of close friendships which last a lifetime. Golf writing is, as a dear colleague of mine once remarked, 'a cul-de-sac but it's a mink-lined one, old boy'.

It is now twenty years since I began travelling on the European Tour to report golf. Although this seems but a click of the fingers the scene has changed dramatically in this time. The season now begins in January but in the late seventies the European Tour was still growing and back then it began, usually in Portugal, in April immediately after the US Masters had finished at Augusta. Although I had covered tournaments in England since the late sixties, my first international event was indeed the Portuguese Open at Quinta do Lago on the Algarve, and I immediately sensed that a career as a golf writer would not be quite the cosy existence I had anticipated.

This was because, thanks to an airline strike, I was unable to board my intended direct flight in London. Having flown down from Manchester I found myself eventually boarding a plane to Amsterdam, switching to another airline to fly on to Geneva and then boarding a TWA flight which stopped off at Lisbon en route to Lima, Peru. In Lisbon I had to hire a car with two colleagues before we drove the several hundred miles south to the Portuguese coast. While this was stimulating, as well as exhausting (this tortuous journey took the best part of two days), it also proved perplexing as I tried to explain to an office accountant why my expenses for covering the Portuguese Open were in Dutch gilders, Swiss francs and then Portuguese escudos.

But then expenses always have been a trial for journalists. I recall meeting Alistair Cooke during a US Masters and the great man telling me his story of how his expenses had been queried after a trip to the Middle East for *The Guardian*. Cooke's expenses showed that he had been obliged to purchase a camel in order to make some essential trip into the desert. He was pleased at being able to charge for this exotic item but less happy when the chief accountant wrote to him asking for the precise whereabouts of the animal. 'As we now, apparently, are in possession of a company camel it would be advantageous to know where he/she is so that any subsequent correspondent to that area of the world may use it for transport also.' Cooke's response to this request was quite brilliant, for his next batch of expenses included an item requesting reimbursement for the money he had laid out 'to bury the unfortunate beast'.

Although I never had to hire a camel on my travels, the coverage of golf even twenty years ago seems remarkably archaic by today's hi-tech standards. At the Madrid Open, for example, we were housed in a small upstairs room in the clubhouse of the Puerta de Hierro Club. As early spring mornings in Madrid can be very chilly affairs, the first task of the day was to lay and light the fire. We then had to compile our own score-board by hand. The scores were sent to us via a wicker basket suspended on a piece of string from a window ledge. Every half-hour or so there would be a piercing whistle from down below and the nearest journalist would haul in the basket and write the scores up on the board.

Making contact by telephone was, of course, even more taxing. It was, however, always fun and although today's mostly superb Media Centres make it all seem quaint by comparison, my own early experiences were also far removed from what had gone on before. There was, for example, the Amateur Championship in the 1930s which went into a play-off. The reporter from the Press Association (a news agency which prides itself on getting the news first) was desperate to make his deadline. Having taken temporary possession of the club secretary's telephone, this particular reporter asked a colleague if he would mind walking the first couple of holes with the match. These holes remained within view of the clubhouse and his instructions were crystal clear: 'If Smith wins raise your umbrella once, if Brown wins raise it twice.' It was a cunning plan that almost worked except that as the match finished on the first extra hole it began to rain so that no sooner had the winning putt gone to ground than several hundred umbrellas were raised at the same moment. Sometimes even the best-laid plans of men and reporters go awry!

By the time this incident took place, Colin Mark Wilson was struggling to come to terms with the concept of long trousers. Born in Portsmouth in 1927, Wilson's career seemed pre-ordained, for the previous three generations of his family had all served in the Royal Navy. Wilson, too, may well have gone to sea to make his living were it not for the fact that the

this and even more mystified when subsequently he was called up by the army and passed as A1. Before then, however, he needed a job. After a stint working in a factory that produced Seafire aeroplanes – a sort of naval successor to the Spitfire – Wilson spotted an advert for a trainee reporter with the *Salisbury Times*, applied and was offered indentures to be trained over three years. His starting wage was 10 shillings a week, rising to 25 shillings during his third year. So Wilson began a journalistic career that was to lead him on to London's *Evening Standard* and the *Daily Express*. First, though, he had to drop his Christian name as there was another Colin Wilson who was by-lined nationally.

While Mark Wilson was destined to become one of the best-known golf writers of his generation, the game was some time in making an impact on him. Initially he made his way as news reporter, eventually finding himself in Cyprus as a foreign correspondent for *The Standard*. The terrorist organisation, or freedom fighters depending on your perspective, EOKA were disrupting island life at the time with the usual depressing litany of bombings and assassinations. Wilson, however, enjoyed this sort of thing. At least he did until the day the terror struck too close to home.

'In all I spent three years in Cyprus but one day a very good friend of mine was shot dead by EOKA and it affected me greatly, so much that I was brought back to London for a time to recover. I was a bit like a spare part in the office and one day in 1957 I was told to go up to Lindrick in Yorkshire and cover any news angles from the Ryder Cup. It was the first time I'd been to a golf event. I didn't play the game, wasn't interested in it.'

This, of course, was the Ryder Cup that Great Britain & Ireland won, thus staunching a tidal wave of defeat that had stretched back many years. Wilson's job, meanwhile, was to service eight editions of *The Standard* with news stories each day, a task that tested even *his* powers of ingenuity and imagination.

'It was hard work. I remember writing one story about a spider bringing the Ryder Cup to a halt. No, I can't remember how it did that, but I do recall being a

combination of water and ship made his stomach heave swifter than even a particularly dodgy prawn.

'The Royal Navy used to run these annual family days when sons were taken to sea by their fathers and I used to dread it because I'd spend most of the time hanging over the side of the ship throwing up. It was awful. I wasn't sure what I was going to do but I knew that after several generations I was definitely not going to sea.'

Having discovered that a life on the ocean wave was not for him, Wilson tried to join the Royal Air Force but was rejected after failing a medical. He was surprised at

bit ashamed of the spin I put on that particular tale.' Away from the demands of the news desk, however, Wilson found himself increasingly fascinated by the actual game he was witnessing for the first time.

'I was bowled over by it all, by the atmosphere, by the emotion, most of all by the fact that it was all about men taking part in a real contest. There were no professional fouls, no cheating and certainly no physical contact but I still felt this was the hardest sporting contest I'd ever seen. I remember when Eric Brown beat the big American star Tommy Bolt, and Bolt said to him, "I didn't enjoy that one bloody bit". Great stuff.'

Invigorated by the golf, Wilson shortly afterwards returned to Cyprus for what was to prove his final stint as a foreign reporter. He took with him a driver, a putter and a box of golf balls. There was, however, a problem.

'I didn't realise it until I got there but Cyprus didn't have a golf course in those days and so I had to practise on a piece of scrubland. It wasn't long before the balls had gone and that was the end of that.' Shortly after his last ball had disappeared into the Cyprus jungle, Wilson returned to London where he became deputy news editor. Although this was a position of some serious importance on the paper, he did not enjoy it. Being 'chained to a desk' was not his idea of fun. What he increasingly enjoyed, however, was his golf.

'By now I'd joined forces with three other guys who were as daft about the game as I was. We took it in turns to get up at 4am and wait outside Richmond GC to be first in the queue for tee times. We always got ticket numbers 40, 41, 42 and 43 because we knew that meant a tee time of around 7.45am. After that, the daft bugger who'd got up went home and had some breakfast before returning to play. By now I was getting better at the game and I decided to join a club. Of course, it wasn't as difficult to do this back then as it is now.'

So Wilson trundled along to Royal Mid-Surrey Golf Club, found the secretary and announced that he was ready to join. He admits he did not know a soul at the club but he obviously passed whatever test the secretary had set for new members and, after a pause, he was told that, 'as you are an Australian, I can allow you an immediate three-month membership during which you can make yourself known to other members and they may then wish to support your application for full membership'. Wilson began to point out that he was not Australian but his admittedly feeble protest fell on deaf ears, and he wandered away unsure whether to be overjoyed at his success or dismayed at being taken for an Aussie. The secretary's plan worked, however, and before the year was out Wilson was a full member of the golf club that meanders alongside Kew Gardens.

This good fortune only served to underline his new-found commitment to the game. At *The Standard*'s offices he finally plucked up the courage to approach his editor and tell him he had had enough of the news desk and would like to 'have a go at the golf correspondent's job' which had just become vacant. His

'I used to go and play against Tony Jacklin quite often for a few pounds. I'd never win, of course, but could you imagine a reporter doing that against a top star now?'

editor told him not to be so silly, that he would be news editor within a year and that this was a serious job in journalism. Undeterred, Wilson insisted and so a compromise was reached whereby he would have a pop at his new passion but that it would be no more than a trial period after which his future would be reassessed.

'The editor was convinced I'd soon get golf out of my system but that simply never happened and I've made my professional living from the game ever since,'  says Wilson. His first assignment was The President's Putter which is the annual knock-out between former Oxford and Cambridge golf blues. Perversely staged in January at Rye Golf Club on the Kent coast, The Putter is a charming, archaic and sometimes anarchic celebration of the game. Frostbite is often as much a problem as a dodgy putting stroke and when the players wander into the clubhouse eventually, there really is honey, toast and tea on offer. Nowadays the week-long competition is reported on because it is such a daft, British sort of thing which amuses the readers of *The Times* and *The Telegraph* but which is ignored by more mass-circulation newspapers. When Wilson set off in January 1963, however, The President's Putter was still a reasonably serious event. It was also, as ever, cold.

'In fact it snowed at Rye so the whole thing was moved to Littlestone Golf Club which is where I found myself shivering over a typewriter,' says Wilson. 'I filed my first reports and soon after I got a telegram from the editor saying, "Your message received from Littlestone here in a warm and comfortable office, current temperature 65°F. Carry on if you wish".'

Wilson was not to be deterred so easily. In the early sixties golf reporting was a very different proposition to today. There was no European Tour, no properly structured professional circuit. There were pro tournaments, of course, but these were few and far between. Apart from a handful of touring pros the vast majority of competitors were men who took time off from their club jobs to play in a competition and then returned home in time to sell tee pegs to their members. 'That's

why all the tournaments finished on a Friday – so the players could get back to their proper jobs in time for the busy weekends.'

Nowadays the best professionals spend their lives hurtling around the planet, often in their own planes, earning many millions of dollars, but when Wilson first began his new career the professionals often competed with each other in Alliance matches, the modest prizefunds often boosted by side-bets.

'There would also be big challenge matches between players which the public always loved to read about. These were serious contests with a lot of pride as well as a bit of money at stake,' says Wilson. 'But there were also matches which, although worth reporting, had little at stake. I can recall writing, for example, about Bernard Hunt playing a whole series of challenges against his brother Jeffrey. I wrote about these as though they were the best matches ever, which they were in a way, but the truth is that the Hunts were playing for a Mars bar a lot of the time! It was all so much more relaxed back then. The players and the journalists were much friendlier. No one was making a fortune and there was far less pressure on time so we could all get to know each other better and, naturally, some of us became real mates. For a long time Bernard Hunt's biggest crisis was the day his clubs fell off a bus and a car behind ran over them.

'I used to go and play against Tony Jacklin quite often for a few pounds. I'd never win, of course, but could you imagine a reporter doing that against a top star now? Not really. Jacko was making a big name for himself at the time although he could only dream that he was soon to win The Open and the US Open in a few years' time. He was working as an assistant at Potters Bar in Hertfordshire and his boss was a tough taskmaster called Bill Shankland. Bill was an Australian who had first come to England as an international rugby league star and he used to drive Tony mad, making him open the club shop at 8am and not close it before 8pm. Tony, however, used to get his own back by taking one of the new shirts off the shelves, wearing it when he went out at night and then slipping it back into its cellophane before Bill realised it had gone.

Right: The usual freezing conditions for the staging of The President's Putter at Rye

Above: 'The President's Putter' – each year the winner's ball is added to it

Above: Two of the game's characters: Muscroft and Platts
Right: Leonard Crawley of *The Daily Telegraph*

'The game was full of characters like that, men like Hedley Muscroft and Lionel Platts who were two northern pros and who were the best of mates. They reckoned they were pretty much unbeatable as a team and used to make a lot of their money from taking on gullible amateurs with more money than sense. Even when they were beaten they usually had a way of getting their money back – and a profit – in the bar afterwards. There was one classic case of this when they took on a couple of Americans. The Yanks beat them but what upset Hedley and Lionel more was their attitude. They felt they needed to be taken down a peg, so over a drink in the bar Hedley suddenly pointed to the incline outside the clubhouse window. "See that hill, pal," he said. "I bet you fifty quid I can carry Lionel up and down that before you can drink a pint of water." The bet was swiftly accepted and while everyone gathered outside to see what happened, Hedley went off to fetch the water. Once outside he hauled Lionel on to his back and then a waiter appeared with the pint. Unfortunately for the American, the water had just been boiled! I understand they paid up although with what good grace I can't say.'

Although foreign travel was limited back then, Wilson was delighted soon after his President's Putter experience to learn that he was to travel to the 1963 US Masters in April. The Augusta National Golf Club granted him accreditation but advised him that there was no room left in the house which the club arranged to be at the disposal of British golf writers as part of their

'I couldn't believe it. I'd been to the

'internationalising of the Masters' master plan. Instead they would book him into a hotel. At least fifty reporters and photographers attend the Masters now but thirty-something years ago it was a very exclusive band that Wilson (almost) joined. There was Alistair Cooke who always flew down from his New York home, Peter Ryde of *The Times*, Leonard Crawley of *The Daily Telegraph*, Pat Ward-Thomas of *The Guardian*, Ronald Heager of *The Daily Express* and Henry Longhurst of *The Sunday Times*.

Each in his own way was something of a legend. Ward-Thomas, for example, had been shot down by the Germans over Holland, had landed in a ditch, found his way to a farmhouse and requested shelter for the night. Unfortunately, after seeing the British flying ace to bed, his host decided discretion was preferable to valour and tipped off the Germans that he had an RAF chap upstairs.

'Pat was sound asleep when the Germans arrived to capture him in the middle of the night. They woke him up by prodding his head with a rifle. Pat didn't take kindly to this rude awakening. You or I might have been frightened but not Pat. He was just annoyed. I remember Henry Cotton telling me as we celebrated his 72nd birthday that he had now reached the age whereby he "was no longer prepared to be inconvenienced". Well, Pat decided that when he was twenty-one – at most! In Holland he took one look at his captors and barked, "For Christ's sake, can't you see what time it is. Come back in the morning, I'm very tired".'

Instead Ward-Thomas was bundled off to a POW camp, the one immortalised by the building of an escape tunnel under cover of a wooden exercise horse. This imaginative piece of escapology captured the public interest when the story was turned into a book and a film after the war, but at the time it just annoyed the irascible Ward-Thomas. The problem was that while the other chaps were building their tunnel to freedom, he was busy constructing a mini-golf course that meandered through the camp while confused sentries looked on. Further, the wooden horse was placed bang in front of the fourth green. Ward-Thomas went to the British CO and complained bitterly. He was all for someone escaping but he did not see why his approach shot to the fourth should be interfered with in the process. Needless to say he was advised this was the rub of the green and told to get on with it as best he could. Ward-Thomas introduced a local rule that allowed a competitor to drop sideways without penalty and the great escape attempt carried on.

One way or another the inexperienced Wilson was in awe of each of his colleagues. It is hardly surprising. Cooke, of course, is one of the great communicators of the twentieth century; *Times* man Ryde was then a straight-backed, ex-Guards type, a natural patrician; Crawley had been a brilliant amateur before taking to the pen; Heager was secretary of the AGW and a journalist whose contacts book contained every relevant name and number. And Longhurst was Longhurst.

Peter Dimmock, for many years the innovative head of BBC Television, believes the two finest broadcasters of his life were Richard Dimbleby and Henry Longhurst. It's understandable. Henry could summon up the most apt phrase in a nano-second to describe a picture but it was his ability to say nothing at exactly the right time that really set him apart. Peter Alliss, now rightly accorded maximum respect for his own broadcasting technique, learned his art while sitting beside Longhurst. 'He knew what to say and when to say it. More important, he had the confidence to know when to shut up and say nothing,' says Alliss.

While Wilson was to become friends with each of these impressive men it was Longhurst who was to prove the closest and most influential. First, though, there was a hotel bill to pay as his exhilarating week at Augusta came to an end.

'I'd had a glorious week. Jack Nicklaus had won the Masters for the first time to confirm that he was the emerging superstar, and the hotel in which I'd been staying in downtown Augusta had been excellent. I went to check out and was more than happy to pay my bill when I discovered it was the princely sum of 188 dollars. When the cashier passed my bill over to me she

also gave 12 dollars in cash. I assumed she was being terribly efficient and giving me my change first, so I handed over 200 dollars. But she gave me the money back, explaining that the Augusta club had deposited 200 dollars with them to cover my stay and that this was my change which I may as well have. I couldn't believe it. I'd been to the Masters, had a wonderful time and now I discovered I'd been "paid" for the privilege. Back in London the editor was in a warm office, but now I knew that I'd made the right decision about becoming a golf correspondent.'

Wilson's debut year on the world golf circuit was completed in '63 when he returned to America for the Ryder Cup. The USA team – ultimately victorious, as was usually the case – was captained by Arnold Palmer, the ex-Marine who had become the father to modern

Wilson's greatest achievement! Receiving a golf prize from Arnold

Arnold Palmer at a press conference with (from l to r) Norman Mair of *The Scotsman*, Mark Wilson, Ron Wills of *The Daily Mirror*, Jack Statter of *The Sun* and Michael McDonnell of *The Daily Mail*

home. She started up her Morris Minor and began to move off from her special parking space beside our tent. Unfortunately, her bumper somehow managed to snag on the main telephone wire and she dragged the whole thing out, plunging the Press Tent into even more desperate silence as scores of reporters tried to 'phone their offices. But then there was always an incident of one kind or another happening.

'One of my favourites concerned my good friend and colleague Jock MacVicar who reported for *The Scottish Daily Express*. Jock is a great guy but he has never liked flying and as a consequence he took a long time to travel abroad. Initially I persuaded him to join us on a trip to Paris for some tournament or other. I've always enjoyed travelling and I was delighted at the thought of being able to introduce Jock to a foreign way of life for the first time. We booked into a typical, city-centre hotel and that evening several of us took Jock next door to one of those café-bars for a bite to eat and a few drinks. After a few bottles had been opened we started to play on one of those football tables, you know the ones where you spin the players round via a handle. It was England versus Scotland and by now Jock was in a high state of excitement. I can't remember what the score was but Jock *nearly* got a goal and bellowed his disappointment loud into the night air. He was even more disappointed when his false teeth shot out on to the table and worse still when one of his opponents seized the opportunity to slam the teeth into goal. By now the patron was taking notice of our rather rowdy behaviour. The last straw for him came when he saw us putting our hands down the goal. We were trying (a) not to die from laughing and (b) to retrieve Jock's molars, but he thought we were trying to get a ball back without putting any money into his machine and he threw us out. So Jock's first night abroad ended with the poor guy wide-eyed, a bit legless and certainly toothless in the middle of Paris. Next morning he could not even have his croissant at breakfast and it was some hours before one of us managed to return to the café and explain what had happened so that the machine could be taken apart and Jock's teeth returned to him. We didn't go back.'

pro golf and whose up-and-at-'em style had made him a household name throughout the golf-playing world. Such was the American superiority back then, that Palmer was able to combine the role of skipper with his rightful place as star player. This was impressive but Wilson the journalist was rather more taken by the American attitude to technology.

'For a start I managed to have a telephone installed at my desk within an hour of arriving in Atlanta. This was incredible because back then it took months to order a telephone in the UK. Even more incredible was the fact that there was a television set on my desk as well. I had never had this luxury before and, for an evening paper reporter like myself, it was an incredible boon to be able to sit in front of the screen and file my reports back to London early in the day.'

By the seventies Wilson had moved on to the national newspaper scene via the (then) *Standard*'s sister paper, *The Daily Express*. Technology, of one kind or another, was still part of his life, however. 'During one Open at St Andrews it was just coming up to deadline time for most people, probably around 6.30pm, and there was the usual quiet and desperate air in the big Press Tent to the side of the first tee. This was also the time when a nurse who had been on duty that day decided it was time to go

hen he wrote a report from a tournament in Jersey that was mostly about the fact –
urse for German soldiers supposed still to be living in a network of tunnels.'

By now golf's appeal was broadening thanks to television and the emergence of Tony Jacklin as a genuine star. The small band of reporters gradually increased to include journalists from the tabloids as well as various freelance writers. Prominent amongst the newcomers was a tall, angular man called Jack Statter who wrote about golf for *The Sun* newspaper.

Statter was a brilliantly talented man and a gifted writer. He once described Jack Nicklaus marching to victory down the 18th fairway at St Andrews as 'like Caesar returning to Rome in triumph'. But it was other exploits that endeared him to Wilson and everyone else who met him. He could, for example, walk into a strange bar and within one minute memorise the name and position of every bottle behind the bar, winning many a drink as a result of his phenomenal memory. He could, at times, drink from almost every bottle as well. But he was a disciplined drinker, reserving Thursdays as his day to imbibe to excess. As a result of this he once stumbled back into a Press Tent around deadline time, gazed at the scoreboard, talked to a few people, made a few notes on the back of a cigarette packet and picked up a telephone to dictate his copy.

Unfortunately, Jack had replaced his cigarette packet in his right pocket but when his copy-taker answered he pulled out the cigarette packet he had in his left pocket. This contained his report from the day before. Slightly befuddled, Jack dictated the words he had written and an even more befuddled *Sun* sports desk merrily reprinted the report they had delivered to an innocent public twenty-four hours earlier.

'Jack was also the guy who upset the War Office once when he wrote a report from a tournament in Jersey that was mostly about the fact – *his* fact – that soldiers were scouring the golf course for German soldiers who were supposed still to be living in a network of tunnels. It was all Jack's imagination, of course. He *had* seen some soldiers on the course but they were merely members of a cadet force who had wandered off line. The rest was down to Jack's incredible imagination. However, the War Office sent over a Major the following day to tell us in all seriousness that there were no Germans hiding on Jersey – to the best of their

knowledge anyway. It was all a hoot. Nowadays you'd probably get sacked for this sort of thing but then people still had a sense of humour.'

This sense of humour extended to the players. For a long time the main stars played a game called 'Noddy' which necessitated secreting a condom in another guy's luggage, his wallet or his suitcase – anywhere where it could cause the maximum embarrassment. Amongst the highlights of this prank was the time one of the pros was chatting up a particularly attractive blonde at an official reception. 'He was drinking a gin and tonic at the time and he was horrified when the ice began to melt and "Noddy" came floating up to the surface while the lady of his choice stared in amazement. The game might have ended there but instead it carried on for a while until the day of a long-driving contest when one guy stepped on to the tee, pulled out his driver in front of hundreds of spectators, pulled off the head cover and then had to remove "Noddy" from his club-head. That, as far as I can remember, stopped it. For a while at least.'

This *laissez-faire* attitude amongst the day's top players extended in other directions as well. At one Canada Cup match at St Nom-la-Breteche, a delightful club just outside Paris, Wilson found himself having to conduct a covert operation under the orders of Christy O'Connor Senior, or 'Himself' as the legendary Irish star was known to his legion of admirers. O'Connor liked a drink but it was during this Canada Cup that he either had a bad prawn or 'one too many'. Whatever the reason, when Wilson bumped into his friend at breakfast time O'Connor wore a distinctly bleary look.

'It had been a very, very good night at the Irish Embassy the evening before and Christy, as ever, had been fêted to excess. When I saw him that morning he clearly was not very well. Unfortunately, he was already hurrying to the tee without the benefit of breakfast so when he saw me he croaked, "Wilson, fetch me a pot of black coffee". I told him that I couldn't bring a pot of coffee on to the first tee in the Canada Cup. Instead I offered to stand to the side of the first fairway, round about where his opening drive should land. In order to maintain discretion I actually stood back amongst the

trees so none of the spectators could spot me. Christy, however, did and he deliberately sliced his drive into the trees alongside me. He walked in, took a look at his ball, grinned at me, gulped the coffee, clipped his ball back out and went on to play a marvellous round. Tremendous man.'

By the early seventies Wilson had forged a lasting friendship with Longhurst. The two lived not far apart – Wilson in Brighton with his wife Joan and daughters Jacqueline and Lisa, Longhurst at his converted wind-mill a few miles inland amidst the Sussex Downs. The pair met regularly away from their joint commitments to tournament golf and even more regularly when Wilson worked with the great man on his *Best Of Henry Longhurst* book.

'Longhurst was a marvellous man, a one-off. I wor-shipped the guy, to me he was a god. Apart from his tal-ent, he was just full of life. And fun. Until he gave up

the game completely, he was a very good player. He used to compete, for example, in the Halford-Hewitt at Sunningdale and he would always order a taxi to come to the 14th green by which time he hoped his match would be over, one way or the other, and he and his opponent could then get in the car and go down to the Chequers pub for a few drinks. If the match didn't fin-ish there, the taxi would have to cruise along as best it could beside the players. That was Henry.'

One day, however, Wilson found his good friend rather less full of life than usual. Longhurst had just had cancer diagnosed and he was understandably depressed. An operation had been advised but as this would have necessitated a colostomy bag Longhurst dismissed such an idea. After talking for a while Wilson departed. Unknown to him Longhurst determined to take his own life. This, he was advised, would be best achieved by taking a certain four tablets and drinking

Left: (l to r) Peter Tupling, Stuart Brown, Eric Brown, Brain Barnes, Derek Pillage, Dougie McLelland, Guy Hunt, Christie O'Connor, ? (unknown) and Tommy Horton

Prince Philip in conversation with Henry Longhurst at the Nine Nations Golf Tournament at Blackpool in 1963

alcohol with them. He must also make sure he was not discovered for at least four hours. So the next day, a bright, hot, summer's day, the great man selected a bottle of malt whisky and took himself to the furthest part of his garden to say goodbye. 'It was a very good malt and I suppose Henry thought it would be a fearful waste to take the tablets too soon. Anyway he was discovered several hours later, unconscious, an empty bottle by his side, the four tablets still clutched in his hand. He didn't attempt suicide again but he did live pretty happily for several more years.

'In fact I visited him two days before his death. It was a Wednesday and I called at his home on my way to some tournament. He was very frail and he looked tired. As I prepared to leave he got hold of my hand and said, "Mark, I think I'll go on Friday. I've had enough". I told him not to be so daft and that I'd see him again at the weekend. I didn't. He died on Friday.' But before then, there was another visitor.

'A very famous person came to see him on the Thursday immediately before he died and they got paralytic on champagne. As they said goodbye – and each knew it really was goodbye – this chap asked Henry if he'd let him know eventually if the grass really *was* greener on the other side. A year later this same man was entering a function in Leeds when a woman came up to him and introduced herself. She was, she said, a psychic. Further, she said she had a message for him from someone called Henry (she didn't know the surname) and that she had been asked to pass on the fact that the grass was greener. The famous person was so taken aback that he had to return to his hotel.'

NOTE: Although Mark Wilson would not confirm it, I understand the 'famous person' to have been Sir Douglas Bader.

Chapter 8:
The image is the thing

'Even the TV commentators are choking.'

Tony Jacklin observing a CBS crew covering the 1970 US Masters

Left: TV hoists on the course at Turnberry during The Open in 1994

Right: Dapper American star Walter Hagen faces the world's Press in 1928

Television

While all sports have benefited in some way from television, golf has enjoyed a special relationship with the one-eyed monster of the twentieth century – eventually. However, until the advent of lightweight cameras and modern technology generally, the game was a nightmare for TV people to cover. The sheer scale of a golf tournament means a production of titanic proportions with many miles of cable to be laid and a small army of technicians to install (and feed and water) in what is basically a very large field.

The consequent opportunities for disaster are also titanic for, though there may be no icebergs, the unpredictable factors like severe weather and a swirling crowd of spectators can combine to thwart even the most diligent of directors. Despite these potential problems, though, television loves the game, the cameras caressing the aesthetic appeal of a sport that is, for the most part, played in beautiful places. And those television companies which rely hugely on advertising revenue also like the game for the fact that it delivers unto them an audience of high-wage earners and spenders.

Nowadays the TV golf teams at such companies as Sky and the BBC are highly trained groups, smoothly moving into place at run-of-the-mill tournaments and great championships but until relatively recently the coverage of golf was a much rougher-edged affair. Certainly this was the case when Peter Alliss first began to work in television. First though, Alliss had to establish himself as one of the best British golfers of his generation. This was made easier, or perhaps harder, by the fact that his father Percy was a terrific player himself. Despite being shot at and wounded twice by the Germans during the World War I, Alliss Senior spent several years working as a professional in Berlin which is where Peter was born on the 28 February 1931. When his father returned to England because, understandably, he was anxious not to give the Germans a third chance with a bullet, Alliss never really contemplated any life other than golf. As with his eventual television commentary, he was a natural and after turning professional in 1946 he went on to win many tournaments as well as to play in eight Ryder Cups between 1953 and 1969. This multi-faceted man also became an author, a course designer and was captain of the Professional Golfers Association in 1962 and 1987. His is an outstanding curriculum vitae but it is as the voice of BBC television's golf that he is best known.

'As a pro twenty-five years ago I could walk through the length and breadth of Britain and three people might say, "Oh, that's Peter Alliss". But TV changed that. Now if I walk anywhere I get three people every 200 yards pointing me out. It's a tremendously powerful medium and it means you have to be a bit careful sometimes.'

Alliss has always been a natural talker, a man who loves to tell stories and who admits he has an opinion on most things in life. More significantly he is not afraid to express these opinions, a fact that has occasionally got him into trouble. He dismisses this with a wave of his hand and the thought that, 'If people ask me for an opinion and I have one, then that is what they get. I'm not saying it is set in stone but I do not see the point in pussy-footing around.' It was this natural urge to communicate that made him ideal television material. First, though, he had to accept that he was no longer able actually to play the game to his total satisfaction at the very highest level.

The first hint that perhaps his best days were, if not over, at least beginning to draw to a close came at the US Masters in 1967. Augusta prides itself on producing greens that are slicker than the average garage forecourt. Taking a dodgy putting stroke to this part of Georgia is not the smartest thing to do and when Alliss suddenly had an attack of the 'yips' on the 11th green, his putter head cannoning into the ball umpteen times, he feared the worst.

'Actually I kept going for another three years and played in another Ryder Cup so it didn't end there and then but it was frightening,' he says. 'I suppose my last really competitive tournament was the 1974 Open Championship at Royal Lytham where I played quite well, funnily enough. Really it was in 1969 that my life began to change when I was offered the chance to move

Peter and Percy Alliss

up to Moor Allerton in Yorkshire as the professional. Ironically, it was also in 1974 that television really got going for me when I presented the first of the Pro-Celebrity Golf series. That started to make my name, and around the same time Henry Longhurst sadly started his illness, and so quite suddenly the boy became the apprentice became the guvnor sort of thing.'

By 1974 Alliss was quite experienced at television. He had made his debut at the microphone during the 1961 Open at Birkdale and, as is often the case, his big break was entirely accidental. It was earlier that year that Alliss was returning by plane from Ireland when he embarked on one of his stories. As usual his audience was attentive and appreciative of the tale but it was an eavesdropper nearby who was to make a decision that was to impact on the rest of Alliss's life.

'Evidently a chap called Ray Lakeland was sat behind me on the plane and he listened to me rabbiting

on. Ray was the then Head of Sport for golf, rugby league and cricket and although he said nothing to me at the time I shortly afterwards received a letter asking me if I'd like to come up to the commentary box during The Open. I said I couldn't because I was playing but Ray said he felt sure I could contribute something to the team at that time and that if I was playing in the morning then I could come up in the afternoon and vice versa. I thought I might as well give it a go.

'The BBC team at that time was Cliff Michelmore who did the job that Steve Rider does now, Bill Cox, Ben Wright and, of course, Henry Longhurst. John Jacobs came in a little later I recall. I played my first round and came in for a chat. Someone asked me how I'd played, what the course was like, that sort of thing. Afterwards I just sat around and watched these guys at work. I thought it was fascinating right from the start. It was all pretty crude in those days. For the most part we were outside with microphones. I remember Henry telling me about what it was like even further back and of the first televised golf tournament which was, I think, from Moor Park in 1946. I don't think things had progressed that much by the time I got involved. At Wentworth, for example, they used to erect an 80ft tower up by the 8th tee so you could look out over the 7th green, 8th tee, see players drive at the 9th, take in the 10th green and see them drive off the 11th. It wasn't easy getting up there either. Poor old Henry and Bill Cox used to have a rope harness tied round them with a guy holding the rope at the top because they used to fall off. Yes, it was hairy.

'Sometimes if there was fog or early morning mist you were so high you couldn't see any of the play. How they did the job I don't know. There also used to be one camera up there and, apart from that the BBC would erect a sort of shed on stilts behind the 15th green and do the same at the 18th. In truth, back then all that happened was that you pointed a camera from a high place and you showed golf. That's what they did, they showed golf in those days, they didn't cover it, make a story out of it, as we do now. I mean at St Andrews you'd have a camera mounted at the top of the Old Course Hotel, another one halfway down the course

Alliss in 1970

and one at The Loop, and you could show a lot of the play. But it was nothing like it is now. Lord knows what it will be like in another twenty-five years' time.'

However rough and ready the technology was, though, Alliss and Longhurst soon formed a formidable team. The older journalist and the still active professional were in some senses unlikely bedfellows but they shared a genuine love for the game and a similar affection for the English language. Although Alliss remains self-deprecating about his vocabulary the truth is that he is an astonishingly gifted commentator whose instinctive grasp of occasion allows him to paint verbal pictures with regular injections of real wit. Although he knows only too well how serious playing a game for a living can be for the chap on the green or struggling in the rough, Alliss never loses sight of the fact that what he and you are watching is a game which may contain small, trivial tragedies but which nonetheless remains a public diversion. Perhaps because he was used to performing in public as a player, Alliss has never been unnerved by a microphone or a camera, using both to draw in the viewer so that many regard him as an intimate as well as an official translator of the action unfolding before their eyes.

'Right from the start I never tried to be anything other than myself. I was me and if *me* wasn't good enough then so be it. Perhaps it would be different now, maybe back then was a slightly gentler, more forgiving age, but from the off I just got up and spouted away. Henry and I were like chalk and cheese, I suppose, but that was good. We complemented each other in our style. I learned from him naturally but I think also that he learned a bit from me. I was fifteen years younger than him, remember, and I was a bit irreverent. Okay, he liked to prick pomposity but he had also been to Cambridge and he was clearly part of the Establishment which I, equally clearly, wasn't. He had had a proper education which I hadn't, leaving school at fourteen, and he certainly added to mine. But, like me, Henry was amazed by television. Somehow it never ceased to be magic to him. Nor to me. Henry liked to have a conversational style and that suited me also. We just chatted away. I have never, honestly, been nervous,

Henry Longhurst (left) and Bill Cox (right), with Bert Stewart, production assistant, commentating at Turnberry 1963

not even back then. To be honest it all came easily to me, which may sound arrogant but it is the truth. Terry Wogan is a good friend – he is godfather to my son Henry – and he has always counselled me never to say I found it easy. But I have. I think this is the way with television. Some people take to it easily, others struggle a bit. I mean I've always felt that guys like Jimmy Tarbuck and Roy Walker are electric on a stage but that somehow they don't quite make the same impact on TV. I don't know why this should be.'

Whatever the reason, by the mid-seventies Alliss was an established star. This, however, did not mean he was making a fortune. His main earner remained his club job, with his BBC work paying him £40 a day, £15 for rehearsal days. Longhurst, as the senior man, was on £80 a day. By now, however, colour television was in full swing and golf was an ideal medium for the new technology. Satellite links meant that even America was in range and it was the New World that was to add greatly to both Alliss's reputation and his pay-packet.

'It was about twenty-five years ago that we started to go to America to commentate on the US Open. They were exciting days. We even got a few dollars in

'Imagine it! Been in America, seen the US Open, stayed in a decent hotel and made £30 at the end of it all. Wonderful.'

expenses. I'd get home after a week away in America and have £25/£30 in my pocket. Imagine it! Been in America, seen the US Open, stayed in a decent hotel and made £30 at the end of it all. Wonderful. Don't forget that £30 was still a decent wage then for someone in a responsible job. Then ABC became interested in my efforts and the people in charge of the United States Golf Association (the USGA runs the US Open as the R&A runs The Open in Britain) also said they liked my style. I think it was my accent, apart from what I said. The USGA always liked to think they were a bit superior to the regular Tour over there. They felt they were Bournemouth and that the US Tour was more Blackpool. Whatever, my colleague Mark McCormack told me to leave the negotiations to him and suddenly I found myself earning $1,500 a week. Okay, the pound was worth $2.80 in those days but this was still serious money. By then I was also on sixty quid a day from the BBC. Mind you, Longhurst always used to say that we should have paid the BBC because it was through our exposure on TV that other opportunities came our way. He, of course, wrote for *The Sunday Times* but there

were also lots of after-dinner speaking opportunities and so on. It really is an extraordinary medium. Its impact is enormous, simply enormous.'

Of course, the BBC was all-powerful when Alliss was igniting his reputation as one of the great sporting commentators, his avuncular, colourful and often cheeky style marking him out from the herd, or perhaps that should be gaggle, of sports commentators. Now, budgetary constraints and the acquisitive bosses of satellite TV have reduced the BBC's sporting embrace to more of a cuddle. However, when the day comes that Alliss's voice no longer graces the likes of an Open Championship or a World Matchplay event from Wentworth, the loss will be obvious. Certainly, television's ability to show ever more dramatic pictures of golf plus Alliss's user-friendly commentary has been responsible for much of the explosion in popularity of the grand old game. He agrees that he has been part of this explosion, takes pride in the fact, but he is honest enough also to admit that it has been an accidental by-product of his job.

'It's been good to see golf grow more popular but that has never been my mission. I was doing what I was doing for myself. People watching golf on TV has been both good and bad for the game. Certainly, television has been responsible for the slowing-down of the game as amateurs copy their professional heroes who, for the most part, take far too long to line up a shot or strike a putt. Mind you, I also don't like trial by television. People are forever ringing up and claiming this player or that has touched the sand or whatever and should be penalised. Almost always they get the bloody thing wrong but what it does do is make the players absolutely terrified of gaining even a minuscule advantage so they are forever calling for the match referee to sort out situations and give a ruling on something that should be obvious.

'It's all overkill now, a fact encouraged by the huge amounts of money involved in the game. A few years ago during the Volvo Masters at Valderrama I was commentating when we had a ridiculous confrontation between Seve Ballesteros and the match referee John Paramor, when Seve claimed he should get relief (a free

Was it a rabbit or just a cunning old fox? Seve Ballesteros disputes a ruling with John Paramor at the Volvo Masters in 1994

Right: Alliss and lip-mike. Plus glasses

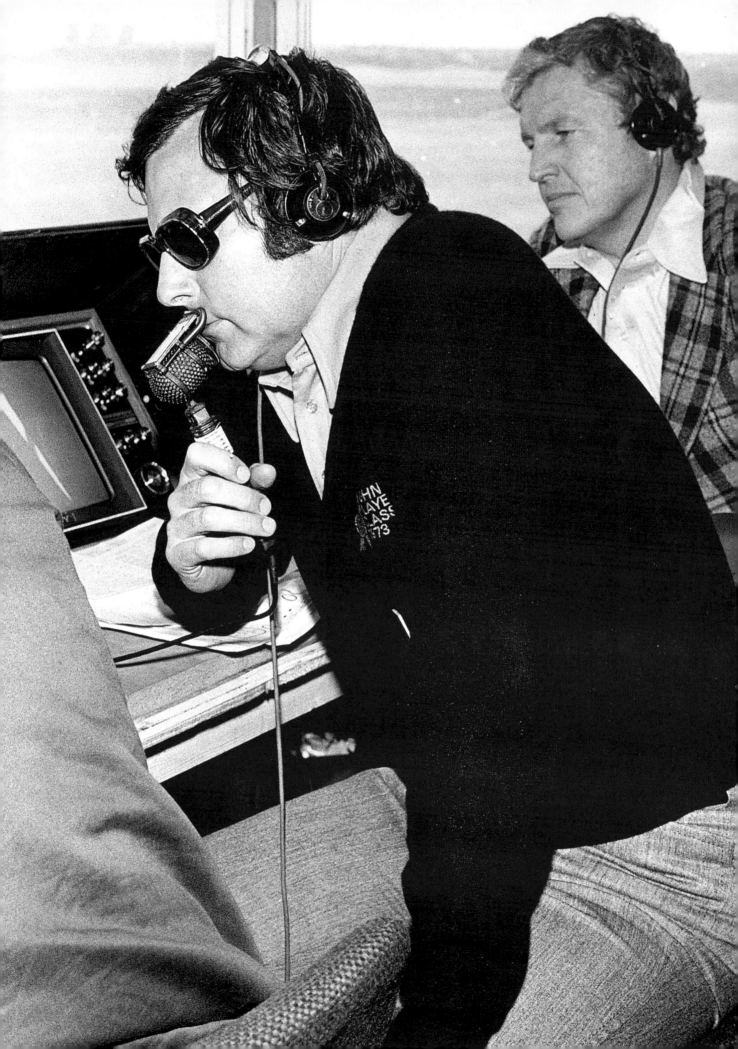

drop) because of evidence of rabbit droppings and thus a burrowing animal after he hit his drive behind a tree. Their discussion went on for an age, at least twenty minutes, before Seve reluctantly accepted Paramor's decision that he must play his ball as it lay.

'It brought to mind an experience of my own when I was playing in some tournament at Wentworth and the pro I was partnering hit his ball into the rough and also felt there were rabbit droppings around. We couldn't agree so he called for Commander R. C. T. Roe who was in charge of the PGA at the time. Cdr Roe did everything. He organised events, ran them, wrote out the cheques, arranged the annual dinners – everything. Today there seem to be hundreds of people involved in running professional golf but this one old submariner

did the lot on his own. Anyway there were no golf carts back then so he had to drive out in his car and then walk about half a mile to where we were. He took one look at the disputed land, harrumphed and kicked my partner's ball away. It moved into a worse spot but Cdr Roe just told him to play it from where it lay and as he walked away added, "Don't call me again, I've got better things to do". Can you imagine that today? I think not. Perhaps it's just as well really but it makes you think.

'The whole thing has changed so much. The facilities modern pros enjoy are fantastic. They are spoiled in many ways. They complain constantly about the condition of courses but they should have tried to play out of the bunkers we had to endure, or putt on the greens we came up against. We used to have to supply our own practice balls and thus employ someone to pick them up again when we practised. Now all that is taken care of. But some of them still aren't happy. I heard a couple of years ago that the pros were complaining because all the free practice balls were 90 compression and they wanted 100 compression. Then there are the courtesy cars and all the rest. I've seen a pro going ballistic because his courtesy car – his *courtesy* car – has been a couple of minutes late, and giving some lady driver, who is a volunteer remember, a very hard time.

'Not long ago I was in the clubhouse at Sunningdale during a tournament and there was a couple of young pros in the main lounge area. They both had caps on and one of them had his feet up on a table. I was very angry and told them both off. They probably thought I was just another boring old fart but I hope not; I hope they learned something. When I was a pro we always had a proper sense of who we were, what we were, and we were appreciative of courtesies extended to us by clubs. It wasn't a matter of knowing your place: it was simple good manners and politeness, and why should that change?'

Alliss, in fact, was one of the pivotal figures when professional golf changed radically in the late sixties with the Touring professionals forming their own organisation separate to the Professional Golfers Association. Thus was the PGA European Tour created.

The rewards of a successful career

play like Jack Nicklaus, run a shop to discount goods like a K-Mart!'

The Belfry Hotel, headquarters of the PGA

It was an inevitable process, for the opportunities for players to concentrate on tournaments rather than their club jobs were increasing all the time thanks to the growth in popularity of the game with the paying public and, of course, with commercial sponsors eager to use golf as a vehicle for their own companies. Alliss was a committee member of the PGA when the split was formalised but he remains convinced that the present-day set-up, with the PGA headquarters sited at The Belfry in Sutton Coldfield and the European Tour cosily ensconced at Wentworth, is far from ideal.

'I agreed with the split when it happened but I couldn't see then, still can't now, why the two organisations could not be housed in the same offices. To me it makes sense to have the club pros and the Touring pros under the same roof along with the Seniors' Tour and the Women's Tour. That way there would be greater access to each other and a potential sponsor could be offered a tournament that fitted his pocket. As it is, they all have their own commercial departments looking after their own interests exclusively. I can't believe this to be right.

'As for the PGA, well they disappoint me a bit nowadays. Some of the old pros used to complain about the PGA, asking what the organisation did for them. I always used to defend the PGA but now I think there is some justification for complaint. It seems to me that the modern club pro is expected to be multilingual, to be able to play like Jack Nicklaus, run a shop as good as Harrods and to be able to discount goods like a K-Mart! They are keeping out potentially good pros because they *only* play off three or four. I think this is wrong. There is always going to be someone in a club who boasts he can beat the pro but all you have to do is say, yes, okay, but he is a bloody good teacher, runs a good shop, looks after the juniors well and works seven days a week. That's what he is really good at and that's why he is a good club pro.'

While Alliss remains a keen observer of, and writer on, the all-round golf scene and his course design business flourishes, it is as a commentator that inevitably he will be best remembered. He has, he says, never frozen into tight-lipped silence when working for the BBC or in

America and, remarkably, he can recall only one moment when his capacity to describe the picture in front of him may have been tested to its limit. This moment came years ago during an Open Championship at Birkdale on the Lancashire coast.

'The cameras picked up a pro called Bill Large who was a very good player and who played at Dyrham Park. Bill had just come off a green when he appeared on screen and as there was nothing much else to show, the director stayed with him as he walked to the next tee. I was told just to rabbit on as he walked behind some bushes so only his head was showing. Then he stopped and it was soon obvious by what body language we could see that he was having a pee. I didn't know what to say but suddenly I found myself saying, "Well, I didn't realise Bill was Jewish". I thought I might get a few letters of complaint after that but I don't recall any.'

It is at Augusta, however, and the US Masters that Alliss has to be most mindful of what he says and how he says it. The Augusta committee are a very prickly bunch, anxious to enhance the aura that surrounds the Masters and swift to deal with anyone or anything they feel threatens the tournament's extraordinary reputation. Veteran American commentator Jack Whittaker was once hauled before the then club chairman Hord Hardin after he described the enthusiastic fans rushing to follow Arnold Palmer that day as a 'mob'. Whittaker was told that at Augusta there is no such thing as a 'mob' and that if he could not more accurately describe the clientele then he might well find himself unwelcome at The Masters.

More recently Gary McCord, whose reputation on American television has been based on an entertaining and colourful use of the English language, was actually banned from either covering the Masters or entering the club grounds. This came after he described the lightning-fast Augusta greens as 'so slick they might have been bikini-waxed'. Unfortunately for McCord, Linda Watson, wife of Masters champion Tom, was listening and expressed to her husband her dislike of such a phrase being used. He then wrote to the committee to complain. This may read like an awfully small storm in a teacup but it was sufficient for McCord to find himself *persona non grata*. Alliss, so far, has survived such dangers.

'One is always mindful of what is expected at Augusta. I've spent a lot of time in the company of guys like Jack Whitaker so I'm very aware of the pitfalls of overstepping their line. It's only in the last twenty-five years that the Masters has become so romanticised an event. It's quite extraordinary, really. It is a private club and yet their competition has become one of the four majors. Unbelievable, really. Their attitude is that if you don't like it there then you can go away. They are autocratic but they also organise the whole thing wonderfully well – even if one can't sit outside on the lawn and drink out of crystal goblets (which people think happens) but out of plastic cups, even if the menu hasn't changed ever (as far as I'm aware) and even if the same number of seats are set outside on the lawn and you

can never get one. They set out to make the Masters exclusive but at the same time present it to the world, and they have succeeded. They never offer a television contract for longer than a year.'

Some years ago, the then Head of BBC Sport, Jonathan Martin, tried to usurp the system when he went out to Augusta for the annual round of bargaining. Martin knew there had never been a contract for anyone beyond one year but as he sat down to begin negotiations he suggested that the time had come to secure a long-term contract. The man facing him just smiled and replied, 'Jonathan, by now you should be aware that at Augusta National we prefer short-term contracts and long-term relationships'. Martin once again signed up for a year.

Part of the reason for Martin's abortive attempt to change the system was the arrival of Sky TV on the scene. The Rupert Murdoch company has been an aggressive player in the sports-TV market in recent years and the BBC's more limited budget has meant the corporation has lost out to its younger rival. It is something Alliss, naturally, feels strongly about.

'The costs involved mean the BBC has to fight these battles with one hand tied behind its back and that is a pity. The BBC has been denigrated over the years in Britain by some people, but abroad it is still held up as an example of what public broadcasting should be about. I look at the past, look at the present, and then I consider the future and I worry that it could all end up horrendous, with swipe cards for this, that and everything. It is all money, money, money and while I would never underestimate how important money is I would also say that it is not everything. When this debate starts there is an awful lot of rubbish talked.

'Take the Masters, for example. Critics of our coverage say that if it went to Sky we would see a lot more golf. This just isn't true. The Masters people themselves limit the amount of television available, *they* decide we can't show the front nine holes, *they* dictate what goes out on CBS and that everything that CBS films we must show. In fact, if Sky were to show the Masters then you would see less, not more, golf because they have to fit in commercials, which we don't. Anyway, why

does everything have to be about more television. I wouldn't mind a bit less. I didn't think it was such a bad thing when television ended at about 11 o'clock and we all went to bed or read a book or got on with something else.

'But then I'm of that age now when I think these things. I'm not anti-progress so long as I actually do believe it *is* progress and not just change for change's sake. As far as I'm concerned I've been a very lucky man. Oh, my life has had its low points but overall I've been fortunate and enjoyed the various stages of my life and career. Certainly I enjoyed playing, although I agree with my old friend Hugh Lewis who once told me that the ideal life for us would consist of turning up for a tournament, playing a few practice rounds with mates, staying in a decent hotel, having a few drinks and laughs and then going home without playing the golf. That's about right. Anyway it was all so much more interesting, I think, back then. For example if I was driving up from Bournemouth to Scotland I'd write to the AA and they'd send me this little route map with hotels marked on it and all-night petrol stations. It wasn't just a matter of hitting the right motorway and droning away for hours. It was more of an adventure.

'We had to learn to stand on our own two feet. There were no managers or minders back then. It amazes me when I read that this pro or that one has not played in an event because his management company forgot to enter him for it or they booked him on the wrong flight. Why can't they do it for themselves, or at least make sure for themselves that it *has* been done? When I'd finish a tournament I'd drive back to Parkstone Golf Club where my brother and I ran the shop, and there would be books to fill in, stock to sort, purchase tax to work out. You did it yourself and you were better for it. The modern tournament professionals have no idea what it is like to do that sort of thing. The successful ones have never known what it is like to be struggling for money. Maybe Ian Woosnam is an exception but the other stars have made so much money so swiftly that they seem to have always been wealthy. On the other hand they have to put up with more than we did. Tiger Woods, for example, is an extraordinary talent and already a multi-multimillionaire. But will he last? I hope so, but I doubt it. The media have him under a microscope all the time. He can't even swear quietly out on the course because some microphone will pick it up and he will be criticised. I can see someone like Tiger packing it all in by the time he is thirty because he has had enough of living in this goldfish bowl that his life now is.

'And I find the amounts of appearance money that are paid just staggering, with guys like Woods or Greg Norman supposedly picking up $250,000 to $300,000 for playing. No wonder they can afford private aeroplanes. Personally I'd like to see young players have to fend for themselves for a couple of years so they can get a handle on what life really is like for the vast majority of people. Of course, there was appearance money in my day as well but I'll tell you what it was like. At the French Open there would be an inducement for some of us to go. This would consist of being put up in a decent hotel – The Celtic, The Reynolds or The Windsor in Paris – and getting, say, £50 in your hand. So I'd go, I'd play and I'd come back with a fiver. It was terrific but I wouldn't have lost grip on reality. I still think it is an interesting life being a golf pro but I don't think I'd like it as much nowadays. Mind you, I am lucky because my life still revolves around the game and it always will. I have no hobbies and I shall never retire. As long as someone wants me to help design a course, write an article or commentate on television then that is what I shall do.'

Chapter 9:
From Hickory to Wallbangers

'Do not be tempted to invest in a sample of each golfing invention as soon as it makes its appearance. If you do, you will only complicate and spoil your game … and encumber your locker with much useless rubbish.'

Harry Vardon

The Clubmaker

Once upon a time, long, long ago in a land not far away, a shepherd was making his weary way home along the line of the shore. It had been a long day, but then every day back then was long and tiring. Absent-mindedly swinging his crook as he wandered towards home and a bowl of lukewarm gruel, this particular shepherd suddenly spotted a spherical pebble propped up invitingly on the sandy soil. So he turned to face the ocean, reversed his hold on his crook and swung wildly at the ball. To his delighted surprise the handle of his crook caught the pebble a fulsome blow, the pebble rising majestically in the late summer air and soaring pleasingly towards the sea. Thus was the game of golf invented.

Well, maybe. What is almost certain, however, is that within a few weeks of this first swing, some enterprising soul had invented a new, improved crook by whittling away one side of the handle to produce a flatter surface, the better to whack your pebble. If they had had a marketing department at the time this no doubt would have been known as The Big Yin. However golf was first conceived, the fact is that golfers always have been just as fascinated by the implements used to play the game as they have been by the game itself. Harry Vardon's plea for players to ignore the latest gimmick is a sound one usually but it has, for the most part, fallen on deliberately deaf ears.

What is also certain is that throughout its history the evolution and development of equipment has had a much greater influence on golf than the bats and balls used in other sports such as cricket, football, rugby and, to a lesser extent, tennis. Not only have golf clubs and golf balls been instrumental in players constantly having to refine the techniques required to play the game, club and ball development has become also perhaps the major factor in the continuing evolution of golf course design. The first golfers experimented with many different types of indigenous woods from which to make clubs, including ash, beech, apple, thorn and pear. Eventually a process of elimination, coupled with availability over several centuries, saw hickory emerge as the wood best suited to the manufacture of golf club shafts.

By the early 1800s the making of clubs had grown to the point where it was a commercially lucrative business so that during this era manufacturers such as Hugh Philip and Robert Fogan were as famous as Taylor-Made, Titleist, Cobra and Callaway are now. In many cases, relative to the values of the time, they were even more expensive than their modern counterparts. Balls too had evolved from simple, rough orbs of wood to the feathery with its leather cover. These feathery balls were prohibitively expensive and so the game was restricted to the rich. Then just as the game seemed destined to remain a pastime for the moneyed classes along

A nineteenth century 'featherie' golf ball. The feathers used to fill golf balls were measured by the amount taken to fill a top hat

Right: Hand-forging clubs

The late Laurie Auchterlonie clubmaker at the Royal and Ancient, St Andrews

persimmon on the end of a golf club. A metal wood might thrash the ball a few extra yards but as I am not playing golf for a living this does not seem to me to too much to sacrifice to be able to look down at a wonderful, polished wood before slicing my ball into the trees.

Clubmaker Steve Clay would not necessarily agree with me. Clay is one of a dwindling number of club professionals who carry on the traditions of clubmaking, and the equally important clubfitting, although anyone who associates this job with a romantic tradition is somewhat wide of the mark. 'Sometimes people think that I wander out somewhere and cut down a tree and then make a club. It's not like that actually,' he says. What it is actually about these days is taking ready-made clubs and examining them for shaft flex, for lofts and lies, and then adjusting them to fit more properly the customer's needs.

Even the most expensive clubs can vary enormously. Sometimes the loft of an eight iron can make it more like a five iron, or the shaft can be much stiffer than it is supposed to be. Fitting the club to the player is more important than most golfers think, and it is a constant source of irritation to Clay and his brethren that players do not take more care when choosing a new set. As he points out: 'It's a shame that golfers don't look at golf clubs like buying a suit. In both cases if it's the wrong size it's pretty useless.' Presumably few members at Clay's club in Hampshire have the wrong clubs for their swing even, if on the day, I visited one or two seemed to be wearing the wrong size trousers. Whatever the truth of this observation, the fact is that Blackmoor Golf Club is a delightful place, nestling alongside the A325 between Bordon and Petersfield. Designed by the genius who was Harry Colt, the course meanders through magnificent countryside, its charm obvious after even the briefest of glances.

Blackmoor has about it that most comforting of traditional airs, and Clay's shop and work-room echo the feeling that here is a place where the spirit of the game still soars above the banality of so much of modern life. Although it is hard to imagine this pleasant man doing anything else for a living it was in fact accidental that he became a club pro and an enthusiastic clubmaker,

came Alan Robertson who was both a clubmaker and an outstanding player in the mid-nineteenth century. Robertson revolutionised the game in 1849 when he developed the gutta percha ball, the first mass-produced rubber ball, and it was this that brought the playing of golf back within the reach of the common man and so probably saved the game from extinction.

The golf ball that was to have the most significant effect on golf, however, was the Haskell. Introduced towards the end of the 1890s, this ball flew so far that for the first time equipment, in the form of a golf ball, led to courses being lengthened and bunkers being re-sited, a sort of early 'Tiger Woods effect'. When steel shafts were introduced in the late 1930s their effect on the game was also enormous, changing the swing itself thanks to the greater consistency of the new shafts. Since then many different materials have been used for shafts, from graphite to carbon-fibre, titanium to aluminium, some surviving, some passing swiftly into the game's more eccentric history room.

Today metal has replaced wood as the material of choice for drivers although traditionalists, some might say Luddites (such as myself), prefer still the sight, the sound and the smell even of a beautiful piece of so enthusiastic indeed that he has been voted the best in Europe.

Born in Alton, his life was irrevocably shaped when his parents moved to Whitehill which is where Blackmoor is sited. Through the long summer holidays Clay used to offer his services as a caddy at the club when he was not foraging through the undergrowth for balls. 'Inevitably I started playing the game. My uncle gave me a set of hickories which I soon replaced with steel-shafted clubs. My parents thought golf was just another of my whims but I was increasingly fascinated by the game, and the pro here at the time, Alan White, used to ask if I could look after the shop for a couple of hours from time to time. When I left school I was offered an assistant professional's job and I did not hesitate before accepting it.'

Clay was on £4 a week at the time which meant that even in rural Hampshire he was forever short of money. The solution was simple enough. 'Apart from my wages I was on 10p a club for refurbishing. That was how my interest started because the more clubs I refurbished the more money I earned. At the same time I discovered how much I enjoyed working with clubs and so I moved on to actually making them.'

Back then wood was still the preferred medium and Clay loved nothing more than to get his hands on a choice piece of persimmon. 'I never chopped down a tree,' he laughs. 'Instead I would buy a block from a company in Louisville which was owned by a guy called Elmore Just. The block would arrive and I'd work on it. It's wonderful stuff and I could make you a wood that was convex or concave to an exact degree of loft so that it suited your game perfectly.' Although Clay still works with wood occasionally, it is metal now that rules the game and it is the shafts that most pre-occupy this meticulous man's mind. 'Metal shafts transformed the game when they came in sixty years ago. Thirty years ago we began to see fibreglass and even aluminium followed by graphite and carbon-fibre. Some have worked well, some not. As far as shafts are concerned we can now make sure they are right more than ever before. The fact is that the shaft wobbles throughout the golf swing. What I try to do is make sure your shaft wobbles consistently and in

the same direction, otherwise you can get a circular motion which plays havoc with the clubhead at impact.'

Clay calls these 'circular motion' shafts Wallbangers, because when he tests them on his machine the shaft slews out of control and bangs into the wall. Although the overwhelming majority of clubs now are produced in the Far East where labour is significantly cheaper, the global market is so rich that huge amounts of money are spent in the development of equipment and its subsequent marketing. As Vardon pointed out many years ago there is inevitably an element of gimmickry to each year's new models. Few are really innovative, but such is the average player's hunger for a club that will make him or her a better player (without the chore of spending many hours on the practice range) that the golfing equivalent of the motor industry's 'Go Faster' stripe can still pay a rich dividend. As to money: Callaway, for example, are nudging ever closer to a billion-dollar turnover and in 1998 they were expected to spend around £55 million on marketing alone. But if the profits can be huge the investment required can be daunting to all but the most committed of developers and manufacturers, with a new ball alone accounting for anything up to $100 million before a single one can be sold to the public.

Steve Clay

The man who took clubs on to a new plateau is Karsten Solheim, the teetotal, ultra-serious engineer who in the sixties conceived the then radical-looking and peculiarly named Ping irons. Solheim's genius was to invent the peripheral weighting concept which in crude terms took weight from the back of the head of the club and redistributed it around the perimeter. This in turn meant that mis-hit shots – and most amateur shots are just that – did not scream off at quite such severe angles. Suddenly, average players found that, compared to their traditional 'blades', these funny-looking Pings were rather more forgiving. Player Improvement clubs had been invented and nothing was to be the same again.

Solheim's original concept meant that club heads became bigger, and now in the last decade of the century they are still growing, thanks to the use of titanium, an immensely strong yet incredibly light metal. And, as Steven Clay points out, the bigger the head has grown, the longer the shaft has become. 'It means now that the average three iron, say, is directly equivalent to what the old two iron was. It is obviously a finite thing but right now shafts are getting longer all the time. It's all about weighting. Take graphite for example: the weight of a graphite shaft can be down as low as 40g compared to 120/140g for steel. The bigger the head, the lighter the shaft, then companies can claim that their oversized club will enable you to hit the ball further. And distance is a marketable concept. In that sense the driver is an extension of the male organ, it's a macho thing. Someone will happily pay £500 for a driver so he can really whack the ball but the same guy won't pay £100 for a putter that might well improve his score much more.' And while clubs have improved it is the development of the modern ball that has done even more to transform the game. At the top end the very best balatas combine relative durability with extreme "feel" so that the very best players enjoy the best of both worlds. Instead of spending fortunes on clubs every couple of years the average player would be better advised to practise more and spend his money on the ball that is right for him. But, of course, he won't.'

One of the great contrasts between yesteryear and today is that we are all much more susceptible to increasingly sophisticated marketing techniques. Either that or we have all become even bigger mugs than before. Whatever the answer to that one, I was enlightened during my visit to Blackmoor to be introduced to a gentleman of 89 who was going out to play a round with equipment that looked as though it had survived the Great Flood, never mind the advent of cavity-backed, peripherally weighted, all-singing, all-dancing clubs. This venerable sportsman told me he had first walked across Blackmoor's fairways in 1915, although he had not taken up the game until after he had retired from life as a sailor, and then only because his new wife had forbidden him to return to the water. Our chat finished, I watched this Oldest Member wander off to the first tee, a junior happy to caddy for him. The sun was shining, the course stretched into the distance like a magic, green carpet. As he creakily lurched in a practice swing both he and the young caddy began laughing. Up above a bird cackled away at some other joke. In that moment I knew that equipment did not matter, nor how good a player you are. In the joining together of these two men, one who had walked this course while men were dying in cavalry charges in France, the other who was not even born when men walked on the moon, I could sense the soul of golf. And I smiled too. Funny, old game golf. Without doubt a magnificently trivial pursuit.

Right: The late Harry Busson, clubmaker, at Walton Heath

The Great Courses

' Neither trench, ditch or dyke made for the preservation of the links, nor the scholars' holes or the soldiers' lines shall be accounted a hazard but the ball is to be taken out, teed and played with any iron club.'

Rule 13 of The Original Thirteen Articles (1744)

Left: America's Bobby Jones wins The British Open at
St Andrews in 1927

St Andrews, Scotland

The road to St Andrews is, for any golfer, a flight of fantasy, an odyssey and a pilgrimage. Certainly the feeling of being involved in a headlong rush towards some kind of freedom, that comes as you hurtle north over the Forth Road Bridge and head towards the east corner of Fife, will be deliciously familiar to any true afficionado of the grand old game.

On up the M90 you speed, sighing with relief and anticipation as you turn off the motorway and head due east on the A91 through Auchtermuchty and Cupar and onward still, until finally you turn a bend in the road and there is the town itself, spread out before you like a welcoming pair of arms.

There is without doubt something magical about this place. Even minus the golf, St Andrews remains an ancient and special place with an energy, a presence, that is discernible to all but the most insensitive. This fusion of land and sea, of ancient university and ancient golf course, of rugged architecture built to withstand the mighty elements that roar in off the water, is a mighty place.

This may, or may not, be the very first place where golf was played but it is old enough to fill the role. Certainly the way the town and the course lie down together suggests some old and wise design. Golfers from all over the world travel to play the Old Course, to experience its unique challenge, its anachronistic, befuddled layout. Here, you just know, is the daddy of all courses even if it resembles nothing you have played before.

To stand on the first tee in the shadow of the Royal & Ancient Golf Club's imposing headquarters is to stand in the very epicentre of the game's history. Anyone of any note in golf has stood on this same tee and looked out over the widest fairway in the world. As you swing that club back for your first swish, you feel the clouds parting above your head as the game's gods look down to smile at this latest rookie paying homage at the

Top right: The 18th hole with the famous Swilcan Bridge over the burn

Far right: The famous clubhouse with some dramatic night-time lighting

Right: Crowds on the Old Course during an International between Great Britain and the United States in May 1923

What you see at St Andrews is what nature has given us.

The Red Arrows cast their shadow over a packed St Andrews at the Open in 1990

shrine. Afterwards, of course, you can enjoy some brilliant fish and chips and a few pints as you rejoin the rest of an unimpressed human race!

The course itself has changed little over the centuries. Except for the widening of fairways much is the same as it always was. Here is the opposite of the modern bulldozer creation with its attendant collection of desirable homes. What you see at St Andrews is what nature has given us. No earth-mover has ever slammed its ugly snout into this turf, although the earth has moved in one way or another for those of us fortunate enough to have played the old girl.

No one, frankly, has a decent clue when golf was first played on this spot but it was a long time ago. The earliest written evidence was a licence, issued in 1552, which allowed the locals to rear rabbits on the links land and to 'play at golf, futball, schuteing ...' with all other manner of pastimes. It was enshrined in law that no one may plough up any part of the golf links for 'all time coming' and so was laid the foundation of the Old Course's unique place in the game's history.

Originally no more than 40 yards wide, a semi-tamed gap between the gorse bushes, the course used to be simply 11 holes out to the loop of land around the Eden estuary, the golfers returning by the same route, playing the same fairways and greens. Eventually these 11 holes were reduced to 9 to make up the total of 18 we are so familiar with today and 7 of the original double greens remain so that the unwary may still discover the heady delights of being faced with a putt of 100 yards.

And then there are the bunkers, so many that only those most intimate with this links may name their number. They are all natural, some being formed by people digging for shells, others by sheep huddling together to escape the ferocious winds that can sweep this landscape. These days playing out by The Loop on holes 8, 9, 10 and 11, you may be mildly distracted by the furious sound of fighter planes landing at RAF Leuchars across the estuary. This roar apart, however, it is easy to imagine what it was like to play St Andrews all those years ago and as this quartet of holes sweeps you round in a circle and gently directs you back towards the town, you see that wonderful townscape rear into view again.

Muirfield, Scotland

Few can doubt Muirfield's right to lay claim to being the most publicly admired private golf course in the world and certainly no one can argue with the thought that this magnificent Scottish links is the most aristocratic of settings for the grand old game. The present course, designed by old Tom Morris in 1891 and revised by Harry Colt and Tom Simpson in the mid-1920s, is a magnificent example of the architect's art but it is no more than a puppy when compared to the age of the club itself, for The Honourable Company of Edinburgh Golfers was formed in 1744.

It was this small band of like-minded gentlemen who first set down on paper the original thirteen laws governing play. Seven of these principles survive in the rules to this day with only minor modifications, a remarkable tribute to the foresight of those gentlemen more than 250 years ago. Coincidentally, it is fascinating to note that 1744 was also the year in which the laws of cricket were first published.

THE ORIGINAL THIRTEEN ARTICLES (1744)

1 You must tee your ball within a club's length of the hole.
2 Your tee must be upon the ground.
3 You are not to change the ball which you strike off any tee.
4 You are not to remove stones, bones or any break club for the sake of playing your ball except upon the fair green and that only within a club's length of your ball.
5 If your ball comes among water or any watery filth you are at liberty to take out your ball and bringing it behind the hazard and teeing it you may play it with any club and allow your adversary a stroke for so getting out your ball.
6 If your balls be found anywhere touching one another you are to lift the first ball until playing the last.
7 At holing you are to play your ball honestly for the hole and not to play upon your adversary's ball not lying in your way to the hole.
8 If you should lose your ball by its being taken up or any other way you are to go back to the spot where you struck last and drop another ball and allow your adversary a stroke for the misfortune.
9 No man at holing his ball is to be allowed to mark his way to the hole with his club or anything else.
10 If a ball be stopped by any person, horse, dog or anything else the ball so stopped must be played where it lies.
11 If you draw your club in order to strike and proceed so far in the stroke as to be bringing down your club, if then your club shall break in any way it is to be accounted a stroke.
12 He whose ball lies farthest from the hole is obliged to play first.
13 Neither trench, ditch or dyke made for the preservation of the links, nor the scholars' holes or the soldiers' lines shall be accounted a hazard but the ball is to be taken out, teed and played with any iron club.

The Honourable Gentlemen at first played their golf at Leith links but by 1836 such was the popularity of the sport that they found their playground too busy for their liking, and so they moved six miles east along the coast to Musselburgh. When this course too became crowded they again yomped to the east, this time to Gullane where the present course was laid out and which a year later played host to The Open Championship (won by the English amateur Harold Hilton).

So far Muirfield has hosted one Ryder Cup, two Walker Cups, two Curtis Cups, four Home International Championships, one Scottish Ladies Championship, seven Scottish Amateur Championships, two Scottish Open Amateur Stroke-play Championships, one St Andrews Trophy, two Vagliano Trophies, nine Amateur Championships and fourteen Opens. This constitutes an astonishing roll-call, one that accurately reflects the standing of a course universally acknowledged as a supreme test of golf. And a fair one: Jack Nicklaus, who

Right: The Presentation Ceremony at The Open in 1992

contained and private, very private. But grand. Very grand.

won his first Open at Muirfield in 1966, wrote eloquently about his favourite Scottish links in Norman Mair's admirable history of the club when it was published in 1994: 'I liked Muirfield from the first day I played it. It is essentially a fair course – as far as golf is meant to be fair – and it has more definition than most of the links on which The Open is played. What you see is what you get. The turf is lovely, just made for hitting iron shots with the spin you want, the bunkers are so beautifully built as to be a work of art. The way the

A 'beautifully built' bunker: this one at the 17th

course is laid out, with the front nine running clockwise as the outer ring, and the back nine anti-clockwise inside it, means that the wind comes at you from all points of the compass and that adds to the shot-making. I've always said that St Andrews is my favourite place in Britain to be playing golf because of its unique atmosphere but Muirfield is my favourite course, to me the best on the Open Championship rota.'

Viewed from any perspective this is a remarkable tribute from a golfer so widely accepted as the best in the history of the game. But if you are ever fortunate enough to play Muirfield – playing privileges, naturally, are not lightly given – you will understand exactly what Nicklaus is talking about. Here is no sprawling seaside course. Here neither is there water nor daunting carries off the tee. Unlike most links there is only one blind shot to play and yet the wayward shot will be punished almost every time. The impression is of a place beautifully contained and private, very private. But grand. Very grand.

Hoylake,
Lancashire, England

The Royal Liverpool Club, Hoylake, is one of a string of golfing pearls that meander along the fertile Lancashire coast and fate has decreed that this particular links should have played a pivotal role in the history of the game in England. Not only has Hoylake played host to ten Open Championships but it also helped give birth to The Amateur Championship and, indeed, assisted in defining exactly what an 'amateur' was in the first place. First though, this magnificent course had to be built.

> When the wind is blowing in off the Irish Sea – more usual than not – the closing five holes add up to the most prodigious challenge for even the very best of players ...

Originally a racecourse, the golf course was built in 1869 to a design by Robert Chambers and George Morris and for the first several years, golf and racing took place on the same site. The clubhouse, a magnificently solid building with a distinctive clock tower, began its life as the Royal Hotel and was owned by the father of one of the club's most famous members, the amateur John Ball whose main rival, Harold Hilton, also was born within a drive of the course.

At just fifteen years of age Ball finished fourth in The Open of 1878 and pocketed prize-money. Seven years later he wished to enter The Open Amateur event (brainchild of secretary Thomas Owen Potter) at Hoylake but his acceptance of cash those years earlier was brought up against him. After much deliberation the committee at Hoylake decided that the age limit for receiving money prizes should be fixed at sixteen and so Ball was declared still to be an amateur.

However dubious this decision was, the happy fact is that Ball later went on to win eight Amateur Championships while fellow member, Hilton, won it

four times. Hoylake, meanwhile, went on to become the first club to stage an international match between England and Scotland in 1902 and nineteen years later the first tussle between Great Britain and the United States was also staged there, a precursor of the Walker Cup. Yet the last Open to be staged at Hoylake was in 1967 when Roberto de Vicenzo just held off the challenge of Jack Nicklaus with a birdie at the last hole.

There may be many reasons for the club losing its coveted place on the Open rota of venues but the most likely is the fact that it is possible to be out of

bounds within the confines of the course, a fact which has led many players to condemn Hoylake wholesale over the years. This is unfair but then internal out of bounds also can be seen as unfair. In fact the out of bounds factor did not become a problem until 1920. Before then a player whose ball landed OB was penalised loss of distance only and so the golfers of old were less harshly punished than post-1920 players, who also had to add a stroke to their card whilst trundling grumpily back to where they had played their ball originally.

Personally I regret the loss of Hoylake as an Open site, for although the course is no great beauty it is a wonderful test of skill and nerve that demands precision golf. When the wind is blowing in off the Irish Sea – more usual than not – the closing five holes add up to the most prodigious challenge for even the very best of players and anyone playing them should bear in mind that it was on this course that Bobby Jones in 1930 carefully threaded his way to the second leg of his great 'quadrilateral', made up of the US and British Opens and US and British Amateurs.

Royal Birkdale, Lancashire, England

The stretch of Lancashire coastline running from Lytham St Anne's in the north down towards Liverpool has proved a brilliantly natural setting for some of Britain's finest links. Nestling somewhere around the middle of this string of pearls is Royal Birkdale, a course that is for many *aficionados* the finest links certainly in England.

The original plot of land was purchased for £5 in the 1880s and although at first a 9 hole course this was changed to an 18 hole layout which was designed and built by George Low after just eight years. Low, of course, had by then already masterminded Royal Lytham and St Anne's. Finally, Fred Hawtree and J. H. Taylor were brought in to reconstruct everything again in 1931, and a crucial part of this work was the construction of the distinctively modernistic and white-walled clubhouse that now dominates the heart of this great course and which is something of a contrast to the original clubhouse, a five-shillings-a-week room in a nearby private house.

What made Birkdale unique were the towering sand dunes through which this succession of designers meandered their fairways. Until then, the received wisdom suggested that blind shots from the tee ought to be the order of the day but at Birkdale this tradition was broken forever, with greens and fairways distinctively outlined against the dunes. Perhaps more than any other British championship course, Birkdale is a place where so-called 'target golf' is possible, a thought which goes some way to explaining its popularity with American professionals raised on a tradition of being able to see and thus assess the problem before them. This, to some more conservative souls, may count against Birkdale when ranking it against other championship venues, but the fact that nowhere in the British Isles has hosted more meaningful competitions since World War II rather proves that Birkdale is indeed a giant. Certainly it hosted the most significant Open Championship of modern times when in 1961 the new *'enfant magnifique'* of world golf, Arnold Palmer, was persuaded to make the journey east. Palmer's play that week took the game to a new generation of fans, re-established The Open as a credible championship and signalled the beginning of a new era for the game. Such was the American's impact that one of his recovery shots out of thick rough on what was then the 15th hole (now the 16th) is commemorated by a plaque. No one had seen anything quite like it in terms of audacity and strength. It was indeed a shot that echoed around the world. But the course itself is now world famous. Certainly there is no finer time to be had than

Overleaf: Aerial view of Royal Birkdale

Right: The 7th hole

Below: The 12th hole in the heart of the sand dunes

a midsummer evening spent enjoying Birkdale's challenge, followed by a fish and chip supper and a pint of beer in nearby Southport town. In that sense, some things about this Lancashire gem have not changed at all over the years.

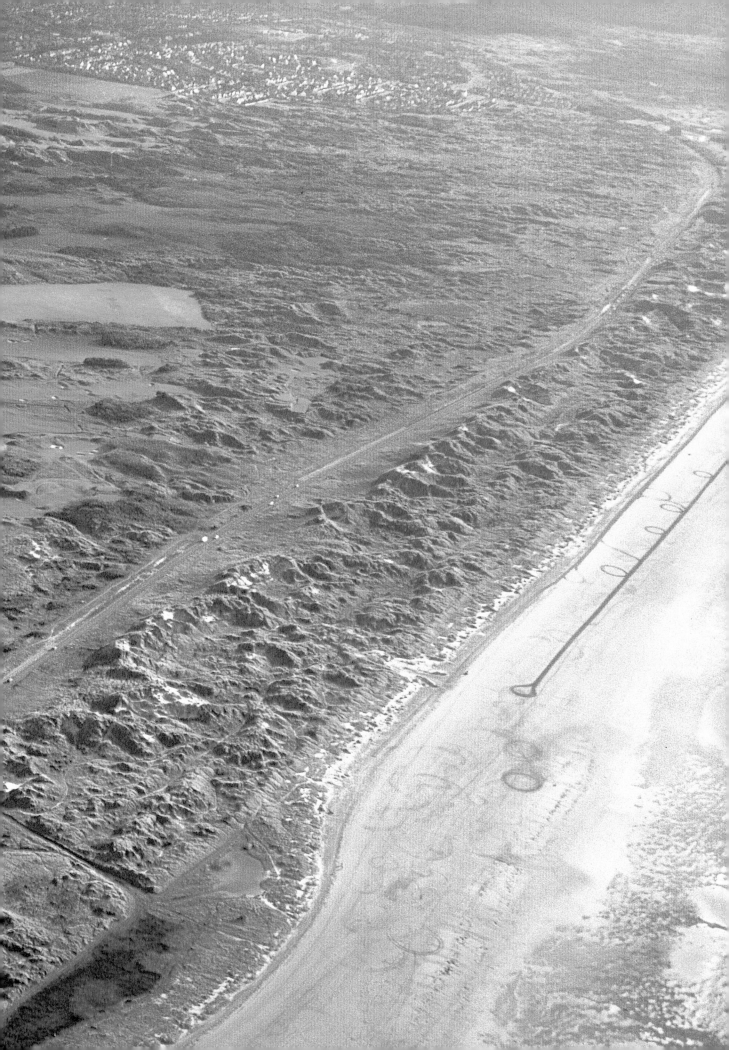

Royal St George's, Kent, England

Few courses capture the original spirit of English golf quite like Royal St George's. This links is set on the Kent coast near the ancient Roman port of Sandwich and its role in the history of the game is now interwoven into the very fabric of the sport.

Inevitably, of course, it was a Scot who was responsible for the existence of Royal St George's. Dr Laidlaw Purves originated in Edinburgh but it was while he was exiled in England and a member of Royal Wimbledon that he came down to the coast and, legend has it, first set eyes on what was to become Royal St George's from the tower of St Clement's Church. The good doctor knew what he was looking for and the moment he spotted this sweeping coastal strip he knew that he had found it. In 1887 he formed the Sandwich Golfing Association and with his friends set about creating a course that was based on the great Scottish links of his youth. Although the American architect Frank Pennick has tinkered with the layout since, St George's remains largely as it was when it first opened to play more than a century ago.

With its sloping fairways and many blind shots, the course is not always to the liking of some professional golfers, particularly Americans raised on the rather more obvious challenge of their courses, but there is no doubting the fact that this is a classic links. So classic indeed that Royal St George's became the first course outside Scotland to host The Open – in 1894 the legendary J. H. Taylor, then a young professional from Winchester, won the Championship with a score of 326, which by today's standards is an astonishing fifty

The 1st tee

strokes more than any would-be champion would expect to take, such has been the improvement in equipment, technique and course maintenance. St George's was also the venue that provided the backdrop to the first assault on the supremacy of British golfers.

This came during the Amateur Championship of 1904 when Walter J. Travis, a rather squat little man puffing on a cigar, changed the *status quo* by using his revolutionary centre-shafted putter to set up a victory that rippled wildly through British golf. Although he had been born in Australia, Travis thus became the first American citizen to win in Britain and the British reacted rather petulantly by banning his centre-shafted putter. There was rather greater celebration when Henry Cotton won the first of his three Opens at St George's, a win that prompted the great man to remark that 'the turf at Sandwich gives one lies to dream about so that with the ball always lying a treat, the larks singing and the sun shining, it is a golfer's heaven'.

By 1949 St George's had hosted The Open nine times but it was then that the R&A decided their great championship had grown too big for the town of Sandwich where accommodation was limited. By 1981, however, the R&A were anxious to take The Open back within striking distance of London and although Sandwich had not changed much, the road networks had improved to the point where it was no longer essential to have a hotel room close to the course. Since then St George's has hosted three more Opens. Bill Rogers, an American who was to slide into oblivion soon afterwards, won in 1981, Sandy Lyle became the first Briton for sixteen years to take the Old Claret jug with his victory in 1985 and Greg Norman took his second Open title there in 1993. Thus their names were added to a list that reads: 1894 J. H. Taylor; 1899 Harry Vardon; 1904 Jack White; 1911 Harry Vardon; 1922 Walter Hagen; 1928 Walter Hagen; 1934 Henry Cotton; 1938 Reg Whitcombe; and 1994 Bobby Locke.

Despite the break in hosting The Open, the mystique and reputation of Royal St George's always remained intact. In many ways it is the English

equivalent to Scotland's Muirfield, with each club representing the Establishment in every sense. Certainly Royal St George's clubhouse has that slightly worn and dishevelled look to it that is so typical of the English upper class and it has always seemed to me that if ever there was a club that would have had Bertie Wooster as a member then this is it. Women, however, have been much discouraged over the years and it is even claimed, although never fully authenticated, that there was once a sign at the club entrance warning that 'Dogs and Women are not allowed in the Clubhouse'. Dog-lovers, naturally, were outraged.

The fact remains, however, that St George's is indeed a predominantly male retreat, a place for men in sports jackets with leather patches on the sleeves and whose schools have set them apart for life. If the Foreign Office had a golf society then this no doubt is where they would love to play. To be fair, Royal St George's is no different to many other clubs set up around the same time: it is just that in this part of southern England time seems to have stood still. In many ways Sandwich seems to have been set in a sort of aspic but there is equally no gainsaying the other fact that the course itself is a sublime and historic place as well as a joy to play.

Royal St Georges, set on the coast of Kent; the first course outside Scotland to host The Open

Below: Bunker on the 4th

Sunningdale, Berkshire, England

While links golf remains the essential heartbeat of the game, there is no doubting the relevance of heathland golf to the sport's advancement throughout the twentieth century. Certainly there is a quintessential charm to the many famed heathland courses of southern England and of these none is more famed or celebrated than Sunningdale in Surrey, where play commenced in 1901.

Sunningdale is one of a number of heathland courses built to the west of London and which together comprise the finest examples of their type in the world. In truth, the discovery at the beginning of the century that rough heathland could be used for golf, quietly but significantly revolutionised the game for not only was it a relatively cheap form of land to purchase but there was no other real use for it, no pastoral objections to overcome and, until recently, no environmental problems to tackle.

There are two courses at Sunningdale of which, naturally, the oldest is The Old, The New having been added some twenty years later, but it is The Old that captures fully the charm and aesthetic appeal of this type of course with its pine, birch, heather and fabulous turf. The man with the vision to imagine a course built across this terrain was a certain T. A. Roberts who in 1898 built a house on the land, having negotiated a favourable lease with the owners, St John's College, Cambridge. This lease allowed the enterprising Roberts not only to add a golf course but also to build more housing, which fact almost certainly means that Sunningdale was the first example in the world of a property development linked to a golf course.

As such it would be significant enough but the design of the course by Willie Park Jnr – twice a winner of The Open Championship – means that Sunningdale represents much more than a mere tick on the

Right: The 9th, 10th and 11th holes on the Old Course

mercial calendar. Park's genius was to create a course that relied on subtlety rather than length, with a succession of shortish par fours that test a player's shot-making rather than brute strength. Originally there were few trees on the heathland but almost every hole now meanders through pine and birch so that Sunningdale seems far removed from the hurly-burly world that hurries about its business outside the main entrance.

Many great competitions, both amateur and professional, have been played here, the wonderful clubhouse nodding its clock tower in approval of some of the low scores returned over the years, but the most famous round ever played was by Bobby Jones in 1926 during a qualifying round for The Open Championship. The great American amateur scored thirty-three on the front nine and repeated the feat over the back nine for a sixty-six made up of thirty-three strokes and thirty-three putts. He did not have a five on his card and the round was immediately described in the press as 'perfect'. Jones himself described it as one of his very best and added that he would like 'to have the course wrapped up so I can take it home with me'.

Many thousands of others have enjoyed their golf here, their rounds perhaps far short of being 'perfect' but their experience of Sunningdale Old more than making up for any shortfall in their game. Many of these rounds have involved gambling, for Sunningdale is also famous for its money matches, at times thousands of pounds changing hands after some complex wager has been struck. Whether winner or loser, one can relax afterwards in a clubhouse that is welcoming and friendly, for while Sunningdale's history and membership might suggest otherwise there is a charming lack of stuffiness about this wonderful place.

One of the famed heathland courses of Southern England

been played here, the clubhouse nodding its clock tower in approval

Wentworth, Surrey, England

Some places are woven into the tapestry of British sporting life. Such a place is Wentworth – the course, the estate and, naturally, the lifestyle. Despite being situated just off the busy A30 in Surrey with Heathrow just up the road and central London within striking distance, Wentworth prides itself on its tranquillity as well as its quality. If golf clubs were rated like hotels then this without doubt would be a five-star facility.

Of the three courses on offer at Wentworth the jewel in the crown is the West, a track made famous by derring-do and BBC television over the last three decades. Twice each year the West is dressed to thrill and paraded before an impressed public in the PGA Championship and the World Matchplay. Severiano Ballesteros has said this is his favourite golfing spot on earth but while the West has the fame, those of us who know Wentworth often admit to a sneaking preference for the East. Both were designed by Harry Colt in the 1920s, a man who knew what he was about and who was responsible also for the likes of Swinley Forest, Sunningdale Old, St George's Hill and Rye.

The man with the vision to see the potential as both a golf complex and a luxury housing estate was Walter Tarrant who bought the land for £42,000 in 1920 and set the ball rolling. Sixty-eight years later another man with vision and a remarkable ability to spot a gilt-edged chance to make a profit stepped on to the Wentworth scene. It would, however, be wrong to suggest that Elliott Bernerd's entrance on to the Wentworth scene was greeted by spontaneous applause. Far from it.

The chairman of Chelsfield property group was greeted with suspicion at best, and outright animosity at worst. He was seen by many members as a predator, someone who would not cherish the tradition of a club that has staged over 100 tournaments including the Ryder and Curtis Cups. Events have proved that Bernerd's heart, as well as his wallet, seems to be in the right place. Under his stewardship Wentworth has prospered. And so it should be pointed out has he.

In what can now be seen as a significant coup, Bernerd bought Wentworth's 700 acres in 1988 for £20 million. In fact he paid sixty per cent, partners Benlox stumping up the other £8 million. Now comes the really good bit. A few months later Benlox wanted out and Bernerd gave them a profit of £10 million. This meant, if you are following this simple if stunning sum, that Bernerd had total control for £30 million. His next manoeuvre was to offer forty shares of £800,000 each to corporate giants such as the Savoy Group. These shares were sold and raised a total of £32 million, Bernerd retaining sixty per cent ownership. So within two years of buying the club, this master of the universe had recovered all his costs but kept ownership. In the City this is known as a sweetheart deal – to you and me it is just bafflingly brilliant. The key to Bernerd's enthusiasm for keeping hold of his new toy was twofold. First, golf was enjoying an unprecedented boom in the 1980s; second, Wentworth was, is, and always will be a proprietorial club. It belongs to someone or something and thus the owner can do whatever he, she, or it, wants.

This, of course, can be bad news for members and as their annual fees rocketed they feared the worst. But Wentworth had become a rather sleepy and faded giant by 1988 and what Bernerd wanted to do was to kick the old boy back into life – five-star life at that. While a few disgruntled people left, those who remained seem happy enough with the way things turned out. Since 1988 more than £17 million has been invested in Wentworth. The Edinburgh Course, designed by John Jacobs, has been added to the scene and a new tennis centre has been built. The courses themselves have been improved beyond measure thanks to a computerised irrigation system.

There is also a new clubhouse, a £10 million redevelopment of the old castellated building, in the shadow of which so many famous players have teed off.

Right: Aerial view of Wentworth

Royal Porthcawl, Gwent, Wales

It is hard to imagine anyone who plays Porthcawl not falling in love with the place. On a tranquil midsummer's day this south Wales course is a delight to play, the sea and the Bristol Channel heaving into view constantly as a player makes his way round this jewel of a links. Of course, when the wind howls in and the clouds scurry madly above your head it is even better. Certainly I have always found something almost primeval and certainly natural about Porthcawl that makes it relentlessly attractive.

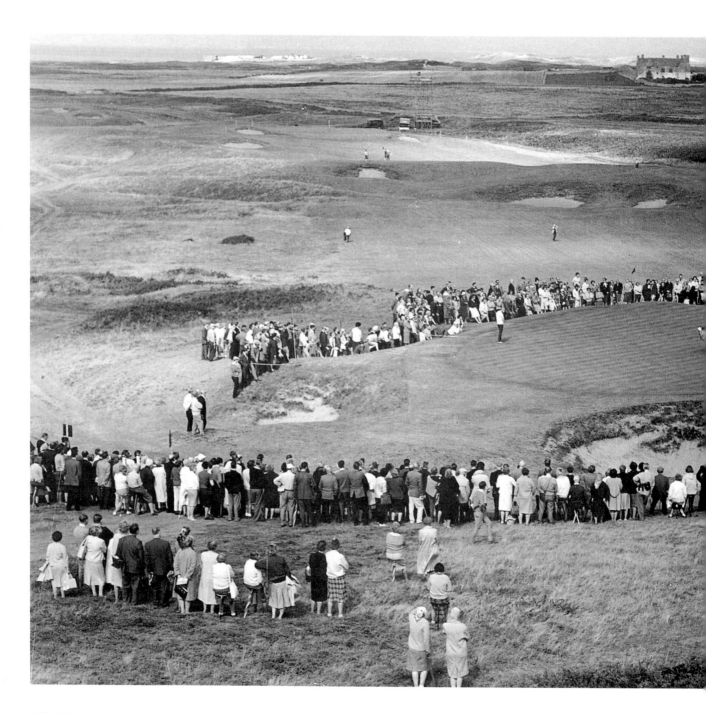

Founded in 1891, the club started with nine holes laid out on common land near the sea but there was too much public intrusion for members' liking – particularly cattle roaming the greens – and a few years later they started again, this time building eighteen holes. The land rises and falls dramatically and, for a links, there is a surprising amount of gorse and heather to add to a player's problems. But there is also a sense of exhilaration to be found at Porthcawl, with the opening holes meandering along the coast so that when the sun is shining and the sea is pounding high up the shore, the course appears to be calling out like a siren to be played. As a course, Porthcawl dips and sways like a roller-coaster, the variety of its holes providing a genuine thrill for those players who like to have to think hard as well as swing well whilst making their way round.

Although professional tournaments have been only infrequently staged at Porthcawl, there have been some, with the redoubtable Peter Thomson winning the Dunlop Masters in 1961 when he gave a superlative display of wind play, while Richard Chapman's Amateur Championship victory ten years earlier produced closing figures that almost beggar belief, Chapman covering his last nine holes in a fraction over threes to destroy the spirited challenge of Charles Coe.

Most recently Porthcawl was the setting for the 1996 Walker Cup, when even a player of the ability of Tiger Woods discovered that this particular piece of Wales does not always keep a welcome in the hillsides. The 18th hole is a gem, a 413 yard downhill par four to a green protected by bunkers and with out of bounds running along the left. The second shot is hit straight towards the beach and, with the inevitable wind blowing in from somewhere, club selection is as important as a confident stroke. Tiger had neither, his ball screeching out of bounds after an ill-judged eight iron was taken ever further left. Woods later admitted that he had never played a course quite like Porthcawl although, to his credit, he added that he loved the place and could not wait to take on its challenge again.

However one plays at Porthcawl, there is always the refuge and the consolation of my favourite clubhouse. Although it has grown like Topsy over the years, the original wooden building complete with veranda is still a joy to see. To sit there with a drink after eighteen convivial holes, the lawn trundling away towards the beach and the sea is, for me, one of golf's great and abiding joys.

The view over the 14th green

Ballybunion Old, Kerry, south-west Ireland

If ever you wish to see the physical manifestation of being lulled into a false sense of security then may I suggest you take a trip to south-west Ireland and play a round of golf at Ballybunion.

It is not that the opening six holes of this wonderful links are easy – stand on the elevated 1st tee and all you can see is the ancient graveyard waiting on the right to trap your drive, for example – it is just that the grandeur of this place, its very soul, begins on the 7th tee. This 423 yard par four runs alongside the high cliffs above the Atlantic Ocean. On a calm day it is a difficult hole but on a windy one it is an assault on a player's sanity. At times you have to hit your drive straight out to sea to stand any chance of it

boomeranging back in and hitting a fairway – a chance that is slim to the point of being anorexic. From this point onwards the magic that is Ballybunion strikes everyone with all the force of a sledge-hammer wrapped in the softest velvet.

Walking between the giant dunes and along a shoreline of wonderful, wild beauty is one of the great golfing experiences. No wonder some critics claim Ballybunion to be the best course on earth. No wonder either that Tom Watson regularly arranges his itinerary so that he

can stop off to play this course on his way over to Britain and The Open Championship. 'The first time I played Ballybunion my breath was taken away by its natural grandeur and its challenge. Definitely in my six all-time great courses to play,' the American superstar has admitted.

Yet the club has had a chequered history since it was founded in 1893. Within a few years it was in serious financial trouble and only the intervention of a retired Indian Army officer, Colonel Bartholomew, saved the day. Together with some friends he saw the potential of this piece of coastal land and by 1927 he had overseen the construction of the eighteen holes of the Old Course as we know them, more or less, today. Even then, Ballybunion almost disappeared again when cliff erosion threatened several holes in the 1970s – only a

world-wide appeal raised sufficient money to shore up the land and check the erosion.

This is only victory in a battle, however, for the war against nature's determination to reclaim the land goes on constantly. This is genuinely elemental stuff but a brilliant marketing campaign seems to have ensured Ballybunion's future. Certainly anyone who has stood on that 7th tee, the ocean boiling beneath their feet, nothing between them and the United States but the Atlantic, and reached for their driver will know that Ballybunion is a mystical as well as a golfing experience. Of course, you may feel this is outrageous hyperbole but if so may I suggest you travel to Kerry in the south-west of Ireland and try it for yourself. If you then remain unmoved I also suggest that you have your pulse checked to see if you are actually still alive.

Above: The 16th tee and overleaf the 10th (in the foreground), 11th and 18th holes

Portmarnock, County Dublin

In 1893 two men, George Ross and J. W. Pickeman, were rowing across an estuary some ten miles north of Dublin when they looked across at an expanse of land as wild as it was beautiful, its heather and gorse folding into the hills and hollows that shaped the land so dramatically. Here, they thought, was the ideal setting for a golf course. Just why their imagination soared at the sight of this land is unknown but generations of Irish golfers have good reason to give thanks that the two men had their brainwave, for Portmarnock has established itself since as one of the very finest examples of a links to be found anywhere.

The view from the 15th green across the estuary

Perfection in golf, as in life, is rarely attained but the 7th hole at Pebble is, for me, as good as the game gets.

Occasionally I have come across a golf course where it has, almost, been enough merely to walk the fairways. Such a place is Pebble Beach which you will find by exiting San Francisco and driving along a coastal highway for 120 miles until you hit the Monterey Peninsula. Here you turn right into Carmel Bay, park the car and then I suggest you just stand and stare, for in front of you will lie the most exquisite piece of golfing real estate to be found anywhere on this sporting earth. Hyperbole? Maybe, but on the whole I think not. Pebble, as this complex is affectionately known, is accepted as the finest links test in America and certainly the most breathtakingly beautiful, with seven of its holes meandering alongside the Pacific Ocean, the surf often pounding on to the rocks beneath the players' feet.

Originally opened for play in 1919, the course was designed by Jack Neville, better known as a real estate salesman at the time, and Douglas Grant. Pebble Beach was a public golf course (although high green fees and a then-remote location ensured an exclusive clientele), that grew in reputation and fame thanks to its hosting the National Pro-Am. Sponsored by Bing Crosby and stuffed with the old crooner's Hollywood friends to play alongside the professionals, this event swiftly became America's most popular golf event when it was televised, viewing figures regularly outstripping any of the 'majors'.

Scheduled to host the US Open in the year 2000, Pebble Beach first hit national prominence when the US Amateur was held there in 1929, the first national championship ever played west of the Mississippi. This Amateur event was also significant for the fact that it is the only one that Bobby Jones failed to make the final in during the last seven years of his active career.

While Pebble's history is impressive enough, however, it is the sheer incandescent beauty of this course that marks it out from the herd. Perfection in golf, as in life, is rarely attained but the 7th hole at Pebble is, for me, as good as the game gets. This short hole is very short indeed. At just 107 yards it flies in the face of modern design that seems to demand ever-longer courses to try to combat the power of today's players. Yet this short 7th, as with the 8th at Troon, commands respect whoever is playing it. With the ocean pounding beneath it and the wind gusting, this can be the longest 107 yards on this sporting earth, requiring fine judgement and delicate touch if a player is to locate the correct part of the green. It is, for me, the jewel in Pebble's crown but the other truth is that everything about the place glitters anyway.

Pine Valley, Philadelphia, USA

In the early part of this century businessman and golfer George Crump was taking a train ride through the countryside outside Philadelphia when he suddenly spied a piece of land he knew could make a great course. Just why Mr Crump thought this is difficult to fathom because the land that makes up Pine Valley is wild enough to be officially designated jungle. This hotel owner was not to be put off, however, and by 1919 Pine Valley was open for business. Sadly the man who saw the future from a train did not live to see his course completed for he died twelve months before the final hole was finished.

Above: By the time they reach the 16th lesser mortals have given up keeping score

Top left: The halfway house and the 10th

Because the terrain was so difficult, the design of the course was radical with no fairways, no rough, no chipping surfaces and no bunkers in the accepted sense because the course itself is in effect a giant 184-acre sand trap. No wonder the course is recognised as almost certainly the most difficult inland track in the world. Certainly when I first played at Pine Valley I gave up keeping score after the 12th hole. By then I had been beaten to a pulp and yet the challenge and the beauty of the place meant that my spirit soared along with my score. Anyway I was in good company, for the members at this club will strike a wager with any first-time player that he will not score within ten shots of his handicap. Or in my case thirty!

It is easy to understand why, for Pine Valley is the ultimate psychological torture for a golfer, with the pines, oaks, birches and firs seeming to crowd in, to threaten every shot on every hole. The sand is everywhere, unraked and awesome in its acreage so that a player feels as though he must island-hop from one piece of greensward to the next. It is terrible but it is also terribly brilliant, the nearest surely that a golfer can come to actually taking on nature at an inland course. Everywhere there are carries to make and the penalty for failing is assured. No wonder so few first-time players ever play anywhere near their handicap or indeed break eighty. One man who did was Arnold Palmer who first played the course in 1954 shortly after winning the US Amateur. 'I was desperate for money at the time. I was about to be married so I collected all the bets I could. I don't know what I would have done if I had lost because it was far more money than I could afford.'

Perhaps because of this, Palmer concentrated as never before and astonished everyone when he completed his round in just sixty-eight shots. So Pine Valley *can* be tamed although it takes the genius of a Palmer to do so. The rest of us can only dream. And no one has ever dreamed more than a local amateur called Woody Platt who regularly played the course and who one day started the first four holes with a birdie, an eagle (he holed his seven iron), a hole in one and then canned a 30ft putt for another birdie. Four holes played at this beast of a course and Woody was six under par. Happily for him, the fourth green lies not far from the clubhouse and Woody retired for a drink, contemplated the way things were going and then announced that he was not returning to play. 'Gentlemen, this round,' he said to his startled partners, 'was never meant to be completed.' It was probably the best decision ever made by a golfer anywhere, anytime. Woody Platt knew that at Pine Valley things could only get worse.

Shinnecock Hills, Long Island, USA

The links courses of the British Isles are unique; nowhere else in the world can you find anything quite like them. In Shinnecock Hills, however, the Americans have a course with which at least to shake one fist at the original seaside courses of Britain and Ireland.

Situated close to the stylish summer resort of Southampton at the eastern end of Long Island, Shinnecock has long been a favourite retreat for the moneyed and leisured New York classes. If their wives tend to be the sort of ladies who lunch, then the male members of Shinnecock are the sort of chaps who spend weekdays trying to rule the world, and their weekends working on their swings.

This is old-style, blue-blood America. There are no loud check trousers or loud voices at this place. Instead it is all Ivy League manners and classy understatement. Nothing sets the tone for Shinnecock better than its club-house. Designed by Stanford White in 1892 this wooden, shingled building looks much the same as it did back in the nineteenth century. Its position atop the biggest of the Shinnecock Hills (more hillocks, really) means it dominates the 80 acres on which the course itself is laid out.

And though this is an epicentre of upper class American life, there is nothing of the snob about Shinnecock. Proof, if proof be needed, is provided instantly in, of all places, the gentlemen's washroom. Here, as a guest or member washes his hands there are two framed quotations fixed directly on the wall above the basin. The one to the left is by Arnold Palmer. It reads: 'Some people love art or poetry or great music but for me the most wonderful thing in life is the sight of a white ball arcing against a clear, blue sky.' The one to the right is by Jack Benny. This reads: 'Give me my golf clubs, fresh air and a beautiful companion and you can keep the clubs and the fresh air.' This, I believe, accurately conveys the sort of ambience the Shinnecock club strives to maintain.

The clubhouse and the course are the oldest in the United States. People played golf before in America but

Shinnecock was the first formalised club and is rightly, and regally, proud of the fact. The other fact about which the members are inordinately superior is that the course was built not only on ancient North American Indian land but by the Indians themselves. The Shinnecock tribe lived and hunted in the area from at least the fifteenth century and now inhabit a reservation less than one mile south-east of the club.

When the land was purchased for 2,500 dollars (almost the price of dinner in Southampton now!) Scottish designer Willie Dunn employed 150 Indians to shape the land. It was some job. As Dunn himself wrote later: 'Except for several horse-drawn road-scrapers all the work was done by hand. The place was dotted with Indian burial mounds and we left some of these intact as bunkers in front of the greens. We scraped out some of the mounds and made sand traps. It was here that the

The view from the 18th fairway looking up to the 9th green and the clubhouse

Indians buried their empty whiskey bottles but we did not find this out until later when playing the course. One never knew when an explosion shot in a trap would bring out a couple of firewater flasks or perhaps a bone or two.'

These days the Indians no longer bury their 'firewater flasks' at Shinnecock but they still work at the club. Peter Smith, the current course superintendent, represents the third generation of Shinnecocks at the club. His father did the job for thirty years and before that his grandfather worked there for forty years. Most of the current greenkeeping staff are from the tribe, thus maintaining a unique relationship that has prospered between the two cultures.

SHINNECOCK HILLS
GOLF CLUB
PRIVATE
Members Only

Index

Entries in *italic* indicate illustrations

PICTURE ACKNOWLEDGEMENTS
The author and publishers would like to thank the
  following for supplying the photographs:

Allsport: pp138(Michael Hobbs), 188–9(Simon Bruty)
Allsport/Hulton Deutsch: pp125, 146
Gordon Child: pp78–9, 80–1, 82(top), 83(top)
Peter Dazeley: pp17(btm), 23, 42–3, 49, 50–1, 71, 107,
  109(btm), 110, 111, 118(top), 120, 128, 131, 132, 133,
  141, 144, 156–7, 166–7, 171(top)
Golf Monthly/**Nick Walker:** pp139, 143
Mathew Harris/The Golf Picture Library: pp41, 48
Hobbs Golf Collection: pp6, 56–7, 58, 59, 60, 61
The Hulton Deutsch Collection: pp4–5, 44
Hulton Getty: pp21, 63, 91, 148–9(btm)
Liz Kahn: pp93, 94(Phil Sheldon)
Derek Pillage: pp97, 100, 101, 103(btm), 109(top), 122
Popperfoto: pp14, 15, 16, 20, 22, 39, 74, 77, 82–3(btm),
  105, 115, 123, 127, 129, 149(top left)/Dave Joyner, 154,
  170, 180(left)
Prosport: pp2–3(T. Hindley), 147(Chris Cole)
The Phil Sheldon Golf Picture Library: pp1, 9, 26, 29,
  30, 31, 38, 40, 43(inset), 46, 52, 55, 62, 64, 66, 67, 68–9,
  70, 98, 99, 103(top), 108, 116, 117, 124, 130, 134, 135
  136, 137, 142, 145, 149, 150, 153, 155(right), 158, 159,
  160–1, 162, 163, 164, 165, 168, 169, 172–3, 174–5,
  176–7, 178–9, 181, 182–3, 184, 185, 186, 187
  (Dale Concannon Collection at the Phil Sheldon Golf
  Picture Library) pp12, 13, 15(top), 18, 19, 24–5, 34–5,
  36, 37, 45, 53, 65, 72–3, 75, 84, 85, 86, 87, 89, 118, 140
  (Sidney Harris/Phil Sheldon Golf Picture Library) pp10
  & 11, 17(top), 19, 33, 96, 102, 104
Mark Wilson: pp114, 119

The picture on p113 is from the author's personal
  collection

Jacket photographs:
  (front cover/main) Telegraph Colour Library
  UK/Masterfile;
  (front cover inset, l to r) Harry Vardon pictured in 1905
  (Allsport/Michael Hobbs);
    American golfer Bobby Jones winning the British
  Open with a record score of 285,
    St Andrews 1927 (Allsport/Hulton Deutsch); On the
    links at North Berwick (The Hulton Deutsch
    Collection);
  (back cover) Caddies to de Vicenzo and von Nida in
  conversation during The Canada Cup, June 1956 (The
  Hulton Deutsch Collection);
  (back flap) Bobby Jones at the British Open, St Andrews,
  1927 (Allsport/Hulton Deutsch)